Pastoral Leadership

Pastoral Leadership is a practical guide for pastoral leaders and managers. The book surveys all aspects of the pastoral leader's role and provides step-by-step guidance toward effectiveness. It includes sections on:

- what it means to be a middle manager;
- developing an effective administration system;
- building and developing a pastoral team;
- managing the partnership with parents;
- managing pupil behaviour and providing support for pupils;
- liaising with external agencies;
- raising pupil achievement.

This book is an introduction to pastoral leadership and provides advice and practical suggestions on how to improve your expertise as a manager. Each chapter includes case studies based on the experience of real schools, questions for discussion and suggestions for further reading.

Pastoral Leadership: A Guide to Improving Your Management Skills will be of interest to all pastoral leaders, new and experienced, who want to develop good practice.

Marilyn Nathan is an education consultant and an Ofsted inspector accredited for both the primary and secondary phases. She works in Britain and abroad delivering education management training seminars and providing consultancy for schools. She is the author of a number of successful management books for teachers.

Pastoral Leadership

A Guide to Improving
Your Management Skills

Marilyn Nathan

London and New York

First published 2001
by RoutledgeFalmer
11 New Fetter Lane, London EC4P 4EE

Simultaneously published in the USA and Canada
by RoutledgeFalmer
29 West 35th Street, New York, NY 10001

RoutledgeFalmer is an imprint of the Taylor & Francis Group

© 2001 Marilyn Nathan

Typeset in 10/12 Sabon by Steven Gardiner Ltd
Printed and bound in Great Britain by TJ International Ltd, Padstow, Cornwall

British Library Cataloguing in Publication Data
A catalogue record for this book is available
from the British Library

Library of Congress Cataloging in Publication Data
A catalog record for this book has been requested

ISBN 0-415-18849-0

Contents

Figures

Acknowledgements

I should like to thank the many schools who helped with this project, either by talking to me or sending me materials and allowing me to use their stories. Without them this would be a much thinner book, because the information they gave me provides most of the scenarios and case studies, which form the core of this essentially practical book. None of the schools have been identified. In the text all the schools are given pseudonyms. Occasionally two similar scenarios are put together.

Introduction

Exploring the role of the pastoral leader is the central theme of this book. I decided to write it because pastoral leadership is such a neglected area and there are very few books which analyse the role of a year leader or head of house. Pastoral leaders rarely receive any substantive training before taking up their posts, few pastoral courses are available and pastoral leader qualification does not appear on the Teacher Training Agency's (TTA) ladder of accreditations, yet having good pastoral leaders is central to the success of a school.

This book is all about how you manage the job of being a middle manager with special responsibility for a pastoral section of the school. Pastoral leadership is a very demanding role and this book will highlight the need for a year leader to be well on top of his/her management responsibilities. It is an introduction to management, which aims to help you understand what management is, and to provide advice and practical suggestions on how to improve your expertise as a manager. For this reason chapters on managing time and teams are included as well as coverage on the more pastoral aspect of the role such as how to manage pupil behaviour and deal with parents and external agencies. The role of year leader, always demanding, is currently expanding and becoming more complex, and chapters (such as 'Your role in raising pupil attainment') are included to help you deal with these important aspects of your responsibilities.

Integrated through the book are case studies based on the experience of real schools. Most of the case studies are fully worked through so that you can see how they are handled and to give you a chance to benchmark your own practice against that of other schools. I have tried to include as many exemplars as possible, because feedback from people who have used my other books suggested that new managers find the exemplars particularly useful. Examples are given of both good and bad practice. It is more difficult to unpick good practice than bad, but you do need some examples of good practice. Some scenarios are included for you to work on. These case studies provide you with some information and invite you to consider what action you will take. You can use them individually or as the focus for group discussion.

There is no blueprint for good management. The situation and the ethos of the school will affect how you should handle a problem. What I have tried to provide is a compendium of possible approaches, ideas and suggestions, which you could adapt to fit your needs, and case studies to enhance your awareness of how other schools have approached some of the issues to which, as a pastoral leader, you have to find solutions.

Chapter 1

What does it mean to be a middle manager?

CASE STUDY 1.1

For action/discussion

'No time to go to the loo …' – an example of ineffective practice

Fiona was always in a hurry. She rushed around dealing with the day-to-day problems that are the lot of a head of year. It was a joke among the year heads that there was often not even the time spare in the day to go the lavatory, but colleagues said that in Fiona's case it was probably true. Every moment of her non-teaching time seemed to be taken up with her pastoral role, seeing pupils sent to her by other colleagues, dealing with requests for information, compiling lists, sorting out problems; there was always something that still needed doing. Her time was so taken up with all the administration and dealing with pupils that she rarely had time to talk to her team of tutors. She was under a lot of pressure and felt permanently tired.

Matters came to a head when, abruptly, she cancelled a scheduled team meeting with her tutors in order to supervise a detention for two pupils. The main item on the agenda for the meeting had been to plan, at the headteacher's request, a new scheme of work for the tutor period/Personal, Social and Health Education (PSHE) programme, as the recent inspection had been unflattering about the existing scheme.

After the detention, when she returned to the staffroom, three of the year team were still there. They were not pleased at the cancellation of the meeting and told her so in no uncertain terms. They were very critical of her leadership of the department. Fiona was too tired to argue. She listened for a few moments, but her head was aching and she really couldn't take any more, so she just walked away and went home.

The following morning the headteacher sent for her. The first thing the head asked was what had happened at the meeting? How far had the new scheme been developed last night? Fiona did not know what to say. Then the head said that there had been a deputation from Fiona's year team about her management of the 'department' …

In Case Study 1.1, which is not based on a real school, the central character Fiona has recently been appointed to a middle-management role as a year head. No one could accuse Fiona of not working hard, but a lot of people, including the members of her year team, feel that her approach to her new role is not appropriate or successful. She simply hasn't grasped what being a manager was about and is performing badly in several areas. Her mistakes include:

- cancelling the meeting at a moment's notice – a major mistake because it affects people's arrangements and makes them feel that they are not valued. This affects their motivation;
- trying to do everything herself – she doesn't understand what to delegate;
- not talking to the team – lack of information will affect how they perform, and lack of consultation will affect their motivation;
- trying to do everything at once – her time management is poor and she appears rushed and stressed and she does not inspire confidence;
- wrong priorities – she appears to spend all her time handling the paperwork and responding to pupils and she does not appear to have thought through what her new role is really about;
- not asking for help or advice – a common mistake made by new managers. Asking for help appears to be an admission that you can't do the job, whereas it is really a sign that you have taken the first step forward. There are also indications that she is not receiving a proper induction as a new manager;
- holding a detention for two pupils instead of dealing with the headteacher's agenda item about an important change – again wrong priorities. This mistake sums everything up. It is a major error of judgement, because it suggests that she is trying to dodge a meeting for which she is unprepared. It sends all the wrong messages to the headteacher, and surely she can make arrangements for detaining two pupils without cancelling an important meeting;
- walking away from the anger of her department – it is always a mistake not to confront a problem.

Being a successful middle manager, whether head of department, subject co-ordinator or pastoral leader, is different from being a subject teacher, although it is often success as a teacher or your ability to handle difficult pupils which earns you the promotion. Your skill in the classroom, and ability to deal with pupils may be what first earns you the respect and notice of other staff and the pupils, but you will need some new and different skills to succeed as a middle manager.

At this point it is time to think about what management means. Some definitions are included in Case Study 1.2.

CASE STUDY 1.2

Management is … – some definitions of management

1. The setting of overall objectives, the formulation of policy and plans designed to achieve these objectives and the establishment of standards for measuring the activity that puts people, money and machines to work in the production of goods and or services.
2. The planning and oversight of the activities of an organization in relation to its goals, procedures and the tasks of its personnel.
3. The name given to totality of executive control (i.e. planning, co-ordination, leadership and evaluation).
4. Getting things done through people, with the most effective use of all the available resources.

These definitions derive from industry or commerce, but this does not make them irrelevant to education.

Whatever the form of words, five *key elements* emerge from these definitions:

1. Anyone with a defined responsibility in a school is a manager.
2. To promote quality in education, all aspects of a school's activities need to be effectively managed.
3. To manage effectively you must have a clear idea of what you are trying to achieve.
4. Only after clarifying your priorities and objectives can you consider effectively your options for action.
5. To be an effective manager, you must be able to manage both *tasks* and *people*. This is discussed later on in this chapter.

For action

Compare Fiona's performance in Case Study 1.1 with these key elements. What does this indicate about her understanding of her role?

CASE STUDY 1.3

For reflection

The main components of a manager's task are:

- planning;

- co-ordination;
- implementation;
- leadership;
- evaluation.

1. Fiona did not understand what these responsibilities mean. Do you?
2. Would you add anything to this list?

Clearly Fiona needs to do some thinking about what her role as a middle manager involves. Reading the chapters which follow would certainly help Fiona. They will address the problems and issues with which a manager would have to deal effectively to do the job well. This book will explain terms, such as leadership, but approaches being a middle manager from the point of view of a pastoral manager.

WHAT IS THE DIFFERENCE BETWEEN ADMINISTRATION, MANAGEMENT AND LEADERSHIP?

The main ideas about administration, management and leadership have been put into tabular form to help you focus your thinking. Compare the elements in both columns of Case Study 1.4, which indicate the main differences between administration and management.

I Administration and management

CASE STUDY 1.4

For reflection

Compare:

Administration	Management
Generalists	Specialists
Passive/reactive	Active/proactive/ dynamic
Focus on process	Focus on product
Emphasis on problem solving	Emphasis on problem solved
Advice	Action
Handling delegated tasks	Foresight/vision
Applying rules	Dealing with issues
Legal authority	Influence/own authority

Administration is about getting the processes right. The features of administration are very different from management, which is clearly viewed as the higher order skill in this context. Terms such as *'action, authority* and *vision'* are used about management, not about administration. Management is seen as proactive (i.e. initiating action), administration is seen as reactive (carrying out someone else's orders competently). This does not mean that administration is unimportant. It is all about creating the right procedures and making them work for you.

For a pastoral manager, sound and effective procedures are vital. They enable you to do the job competently. In Case Study 1.1, Fiona is described as spending much of her time making lists. A pastoral manager certainly has to produce and manage a lot of lists, but in this case study the tail appears to be wagging the dog. The lists are not important in themselves – you do not make lists for their own sake. The nature of a pastoral leader's job necessitates that all the administration functions efficiently and that the time spent on such things as making lists is kept to a minimum. Getting the right procedures set up, so that you can spend your time dealing with the urgent or really serious problems, is vital to your success. Making sure that procedures work is also very important. Indeed, it is precisely this element which helps create the success/failure expectation for any new initiatives you introduce. This means that the time you spend creating effective procedures should pay dividends, as once the procedures are in place you should be able to rely on them. Advice for dealing with administration and strategies for time management may be found in Chapter 3 'Effective administration'.

A quality manager has to deal effectively with both tasks and people. Good administration is about managing the tasks effectively. In Case Study 1.1 Fiona is not succeeding in dealing with tasks, she has no time available to be able to deal properly with managing the people in her team, and leadership is all about managing people.

One of your main roles as a manager is to provide leadership. You will have noticed that I gave you several definitions of management. I cannot, however, provide a clear and concise definition of leadership. Indeed, one of the problems of distinguishing between leadership and management is that there is no simple definition of leadership.

CASE STUDY 1.5

For reflection

The best definition that I have seen comes from Peters and Waterman (1982). It stretches to several lines, but encapsulates what good leadership is about: *'... being visible when things go awry, and invisible when they are working well, it is building a loyal team, that speaks more or less with one voice. It's listening carefully most of the time ... It's being tough when necessary, and it's the occasional naked use of power ...'.*

To help you focus on what leadership is about I shall use a series of comparisons – Case Study 1.4 compares administration with management, Case Study 1.6 compares management with leadership. They are not my lists, nor are they the work of the same person, but they fit together quite well. Notice the pecking order – leadership is clearly seen as the highest order skill.

One of the central issues is to try to clarify whether leadership is just another word, which means the same as management, or whether, in important respects, it differs from management.

CASE STUDY 1.6

For reflection

What is the difference between leadership and management?

Manager	*Leader*
Administers	Innovates
Maintains	Develops
Accepts the status quo	Challenges the status quo
Initiates	Originates
Focuses on systems	Focuses on people
Takes the short-term view	Takes the long-term view
Eyes the bottom line	Eyes the horizon
Relies on control	Inspires trust
Asks how and when	Asks why and what
Is the classic good soldier	Is his/her own person
Does things right	Does the right thing

Source: Bennis and Nannus (1985).

The list in Case Study 1.6 comes from an American source, but makes some good comparisons between leadership and management, which are as relevant for a British manager as for an American. In this list there are some striking differences between leadership and management. Notice particularly the language used. Management is 'good', but now leadership is better, and is visibly seen as the higher order skill. For example, to be described as a good soldier is condescending, whereas, in this context, to be his or her own person is clearly a compliment. Similarly the manager 'eyes the bottom line', whereas the leader 'eyes the horizon', which, as long as you don't fall over, must be better. Words such as 'innovates', 'challenges' and 'inspires' are used to describe leadership and there is an emphasis on success with people. It is almost surprising that the word *charisma* is not used.

Although the right leadership is essential to good management, I view management as the overarching skill, and administration and leadership as aspects of management. I must stress that this is a personal view based on my own experience as a manager. Leadership does, however, seem to me to be the most important management skill, because unless you provide quality leadership, you cannot succeed as a manager. I view leadership as being essentially about managing people and making them want to participate in the vision/team, and about getting people to do things and I see leadership as being affected and influenced by four components:

- the leader;
- the led;
- the task;
- the situation.

Chapter 2 'What style of manager are you?', explores the influences on leadership.

John Adair's 'action centred leadership' (Adair 1988) is a way of looking at leadership from another perspective. John Adair has made a very significant contribution to management theory. His work is not new, but it is still relevant. Originally a lecturer at Sandhurst Military Academy, over the years he has developed and extended his theory. His ideas have been used extensively by the Industrial Society, and you will find them included in the programme of most management courses. They are very useful in focusing your thinking about the leadership roles and are also helpful in focusing your thoughts on your role as a co-ordinator. The interlocking circles (Figure 1.1) help you to realize that you need to deal with both tasks and people and that your responsibility for people covers two areas – teams and individuals. The functions for each component are also described. The leader's checklist is based on this approach and can be a useful checklist. 'Purpose, Process and People' is another way of looking at this list, which I find helpful.

Figure 1.1 John Adair's three-circle model of leadership.

CASE STUDY 1.7

For reflection

A leader's checklist based on Adair's principles

Key actions	Task	Team	Individual
Define objectives	Identify task and constraints	Involve team	Clarify objectives
		Share commitment	Gain acceptance
Plan	Establish priorities	Consult	Assess skills
	Check resources	Encourage ideas/actions	Set targets
	Decide	Develop suggestions	Delegate
	Set standards	Structure	

Brief	Brief the team	Answer questions	Listen
	Check understanding	Obtain feedback	Enthuse
Support/monitor	Report progress	Co-ordinate	Advise
	Maintain standards	Reconcile conflict	Assist/reassure
	Discipline		Recognize effort
			Counsel
Evaluate	Summarize progress	Recognize success	Assess performance
	Review objectives	Learn from failure	Appraise
	Replan if necessary		Guide and train

For reflection

You may want to compare the list given here with Case Study 1.3 'The main components of a manager's task'.

Task functions:
- Defining the task
- Making a plan
- Allocating work and resources
- Controlling quality
- Checking performance against the plan
- Adjusting the plan

Group functions:
- Setting standards
- Maintaining discipline
- Building team spirit
- Encouraging, motivating, giving a sense of purpose
- Appointing subleaders
- Ensuring communications within the group
- Training the group

Individual functions:
- Attending to personal problems
- Praising individuals
- Giving status
- Recognizing and using individual abilities
- Training the individual

Figure 1.2 Leadership functions.

One of your main roles as a pastoral manager is to provide leadership for your year team, both by your own example and by the vision that you develop in partnership with the team members.

Now that we are clearer about administration and leadership, it is time to look again at management and to think about the management skills that you will need as a pastoral manager.

WHAT ARE THE MANAGEMENT SKILLS?

There are many ways of ordering these skills. What is important is not to over-complicate things. For this reason I summarize them as six skills. There is no set order.

Thinking skills Assimilating information, analytical skills, problem-solving skills.

The planning skills The ability to set goals and objectives for the team and to work out how to achieve the goals.

Interpersonal skills Dealing with people: teambuilding, motivating, delegating, or counselling.

Communicating Making it clear to people what the vision means (sharing the vision), what the expectations are and what is going on. It is particularly important to communicate fully with all members of the team; otherwise you appear to have favourites or to have secrets.

Leadership Responsibility taking, willingness to use your initiative and take on new areas, making judgements and choices, risk taking.

Achieving The ability to get the result/s that you want.

There are some born leaders or managers, but most of us have to learn the skills, usually on the job. In Case Study 1.1, Fiona has a particularly steep learning curve and, when I lead a pastoral course, I am sometimes asked, 'Is it possible for her to retrieve the situation? Can she do it?' The answer has to be 'Yes', but that it will take time and it will be very difficult.

If she is to retrieve the situation, the first thing that she must do is to admit that she has got it wrong and apologize to the team members for wasting their time and ignoring them. Unless she does this, she cannot begin to put things right with the team. Normally, at this stage, someone asks, 'Isn't it dangerous to admit to mistakes?' Obviously, if you want to inspire confidence in your leadership, you should not do this too often, but it is important not to be seen to be passing the buck when things go wrong. After the initial apology, it will be her ongoing management of the department that will be the test of whether or not she has learnt from her mistakes. If she is really brave, at the end of the year she will try the evaluation exercise, which appears in Figure 1.3. The judgement of her team members will tell her clearly if she has improved and which areas still need improvement. The majority of the team will respect her for learning from her mistakes and letting them evaluate her performance.

Willingness to take part in upwards evaluation and to act on what it indicates about your performance is a significant mark of a quality manager.

Measuring your own competency in the management skills

You will find that you have more ability in some areas than in others and that you will need to firm up the areas in which you have least natural talent.

How do you know or find out which skills you have?

The exercise, which appears in Figure 1.3, revisits the management skills, but uses some different terminology. It is intended to help you appraise yourself as a manager. You grade yourself on a 1–5 scale and get members of the team to grade you. The top mark is 1 and 5 is the lowest. The first thing that the exercise will tell you is whether your perception of yourself matches that of the members of your team. When should you do this exercise? The answer will vary

	Grades 1–5	Examples
Interpersonal		
Leading		
Communicating		
Motivating		
Liaising		
Guiding		
Supervising		
Informational		
Disseminator		
Spokesperson		
Organizer		
Controller		
Decisional		
Entrepreneur		
Disturbance handler		
Planner		
Resourcer		
Negotiator		
Exemplar		
Professional values		
Teaching		
Goal setter		
Evaluator		

Figure 1.3 Managerial roles: personal competencies list.

according to your circumstances and your relationship with the team. If you are having difficulty establishing yourself with your team, you do not want to play into their hands by giving them a stick, with which to beat you! On the other hand, fairly soon after you take up the post, you could well want to find out what you do well and what you need to learn. You may also want to find out if you have improved over time and do the test again, say 18 months later.

Your approach can also make a difference. Everard and Morris (1990) have a nice comparison of the positive and the negative manager. You may want to think about where you fit.

CASE STUDY 1.8

For reflection

Positive and negative management

The positive manager	*The negative manager*
Acts	Is a victim
Accepts responsibility	Blames others
Is objective	Is subjective
Listens and responds	Rejects suggestions
Proposes solutions	Criticises
Delegates	Is incapable of delegation
Sees opportunities	Sees threats
Has breadth of vision	Is preoccupied with detail
Faces up to problems	Conceals problems
Confronts the source of the problem	Talks about the source of the problem
Learns	Is taught
Has foresight	Has hindsight

Source: Everard and Morris (1990).

WHAT ARE YOUR RESPONSIBILITIES AS A PASTORAL MANAGER?

So far, I have talked in general terms about what it means to be a manager, and what I have said could equally apply to both pastoral and departmental management. Now it is time to home in specifically on pastoral management. I shall start this section by considering what the main differences are between departmental and pastoral management.

What are the main differences between departmental and pastoral management?

This is my list, which I have compiled as a result of my own experience, and you may wish to add to it. I feel strongly, having had both departmental and pastoral experience, that the pastoral leader has to be the more efficient manager. It is worth noting that the point about technical expertise and learning on the hoof could affect your confidence, if people challenge your judgement or you have to deal with difficult issues.

You have to be a better manager. Why do I think this?

Lack of substantial training

You may not have the technical expertise (i.e. you are a geography teacher), who has become a head of year, and you have had to build up the pastoral skills on the job, and while managing a section. Substantial courses for pastoral leaders are still rare. Occasionally I meet people who have completed a unit on pastoral leadership in conjunction with the local university, but this is rare. Your training will probably have been gained by attending the occasional 1-day course, whereas you studied your subject to degree level. The long course, most likely to have been followed by pastoral leaders, is a counselling course. These tend to be twilight sessions held over a number of weeks at a local centre. They involve assignments and do carry credits or certification. The problem with following a counselling course, however, is that it adds considerably to your workload, while only dealing with one small aspect of your job.

Crisis management

A lot of your work is crisis management, so you have to be a very good manager of time and not flap in a crisis. However much you plan, and however good a time manager you are, you cannot anticipate the pastoral crises that occur. A major crisis needs full and immediate attention. This means that any plans you may have made (e.g. about how your day is to be managed) frequently have to go by the board. It also involves using your judgement in making decisions, not only about what to prioritize, but also about how to deal with the crisis.

Stress

The job is physically demanding – tiring and stressful. When you are in school, people, both staff and pupils are coming to you regularly with their problems. If you gain a reputation as a good listener, this aspect of your job can grow and grow. Not only is this very time consuming, but it is also extremely stressful for you, because people are unloading their problems onto you all the time, and some of these can be both complex and difficult. At the end of the day is there anyone who you can unload to, or do you have to take the whole load home with you? In addition, you still have your academic teaching commitment, with its attendant preparation and marking, and this puts you under yet more pressure.

A difficult relationship with your subject department

The relationship with your subject department can be a problem and often needs very sensitive handling. Heads of Departments (HoDs) frequently complain about the year heads, etc. in their departments not pulling their weight, and this creates an additional tension for you. It is almost impossible for you to do academic work, especially marking, in your free periods at school. This means not only do you have to do all your preparation and marking at home, but it also makes it difficult for you to make a full and quality contribution to the department, and, in turn, this gives the impression that you do not care. The worst scenario can occur if you happen to have your own subject head of department in your year team, because it can put your relationship with your subject manager under pressure, particularly if the person is not your most co-operative tutor.

Burden of administration

A heavy administrative demand is common to middle-management positions whether you are a HoD or a Head of Year (HoY), but for you it comes on top of all the other demands. You have a lot of administrative detail to deal with on a regular basis, much of which (e.g. absences) has to be followed up, sometimes by other people. You have to be able to supply information, which may have to be used to provide evidence to determine how a pupil should be treated. All of this means that your record system has to be accurate and up to date. You have to have your records in good order and your team have to provide you with the information that you need.

Unwilling team

You have to teambuild in difficult circumstances. For a start, you rarely get much choice about membership of the team. Teachers are selected for their subject skills, not for their potential contribution to the pastoral system. How the school allocates teachers to year or house teams and how much you, as the team leader, are consulted about this process varies. In some schools the senior management team decide, in others the leader is asked what s/he feels about the proposed team. In a small number of schools, the leader is asked to make suggestions about whom s/he wants on the team. In some schools the team is changed on an annual or 2-yearly basis, in others the intention is that the team progresses up the school with the group until the end of year 11. How much you can influence events also depends on your own personal and position power. All this affects your freedom in constructing a quality team.

Moreover, being a member of your team is not the most important thing for most of the team members. They are already members of a subject team, and this is what really matters to them. All too frequently, they regard their pastoral duties as yet another burden and have to be persuaded to attend your meetings, or find excuses not to come. Although in practice many make a considerable input, largely because they are persuaded by the needs or demands of the pupils, really good tutoring is rare and form tutors receive even less training than pastoral leaders. This makes your task as a manager much more difficult than that of the subject leader, who can expect some enthusiasm for the task. Creating, managing and developing your team is discussed fully in Chapters 4 and 5.

Status

In some schools your status as a middle manager is not really recognized and the year head is regarded as less important than the head of a subject department. Even if technically you are on the same salary scale as the HoD, you may actually have less influence. This makes your position difficult, and affects both your confidence and your expectations.

People skills

You need highly developed interpersonal and communication skills to interact successfully with your team, parents and outsiders. You probably meet more outsiders than HoDs, and have to be able to interact successfully with a range of different audiences. Communication is always an issue in large organizations as very often people claim that communications are not as good as they should be. As a middle manager, you have an important role in ensuring that information is communicated clearly. Your team have a right to know what is expected of them and what is going on. Most information must be shared with all, otherwise you are creating an elite within the team, or giving out the message that there are secrets which some people know and in which others do not share. Often it turns out that there is no secret, but poor communication skills on the part of the leader have given some members of the team the wrong impression.

For all these reasons it is vital to your success that you have good management skills. Most of the issues touched on in this section will be fully developed in the chapters that follow, pastoral problems and scenarios will be explored and practical advice offered.

WHAT ARE YOUR MAIN ROLES AND RESPONSIBILITIES AS A PASTORAL LEADER?

In Case Study 1.1, it was clear that Fiona, a newly appointed year leader, had not thought through what her job was about and what her priorities should be. I shall end this chapter by creating a job description for her, which defines a pastoral manager's role and responsibilities. Notice that it is strategic (i.e. divided according to major areas of responsibility). You may wish to compare it with your own job description.

CASE STUDY 1.9

Exemplar: creating a job description for Fiona

A year leader's job description

Role description – year leader

The year leader is responsible to the senior management team for all pastoral matters in connection with his/her year group. The following duties and responsibilities cover the main areas of this post.

Year leaders will be involved managing a number of overlapping areas. These are:

1. providing a positive learning environment for the pupils in the year group;
2. leading and developing a team of year tutors;
3. monitoring student progress and behaviour;
4. developing year-group activities, including the Personal, Social and Health Education (PSHE) programme;
5. ensuring effective communication of information.

General principles

The following points are crucial to the role of a year leader:

1. year leaders should be aware of and work in support of the ethos, pastoral policy and aims of the school;
2. the pastoral co-ordinator is the line manager of all year leaders.

1 Providing a positive learning environment for the pupils in the year group

Responsibilities include:

- developing the pastoral policy and ethos for your year group – in line with the school's pastoral policy and mission statement – promoting a year team approach which will enable all students to develop their academic and social capabilities to the fullest extent;
- dealing with issues of health and safety;
- providing pastoral care for the pupils – so that they receive maximum benefit from the education provided by the school.

2 Leading and developing a team of year tutors

It is your responsibility to build the year ethos and team spirit and give effective leadership to the tutor team. It is vital that form tutors see themselves as part of:

- the school pastoral team;
- a year-group tutor team.

To this end, your responsibilities as team leader include: (a) *holding regular tutor team meetings* to ensure that form tutors understand the policies of the school on all relevant matters and to discuss specific year-group issues; for example:

- review pupil progress – whole year group or individuals;
- where relevant, review existing systems and suggest modifications or improvements to them;
- pool and develop ideas for year-group activities;
- review and develop the PSHE programme.

Twice termly tutor team meetings are built into the meetings cycle. Short ad hoc meetings may be necessary occasionally to deal with the particular issues which arise.

(b) *Developing the team.* This includes:

- monitoring, evaluating and providing feedback on the performance of members of the tutor team;
- leading or providing training, which will enable members of the team to develop in their role as tutors.

3 Monitoring student progress and behaviour

Year leaders will work together with form tutors and the pastoral co-ordinator to ensure that effective systems are in place for monitoring pupil progress and that they are communicated to all those involved. This will involve *holding a short weekly meeting with each tutor*, ca. 15 minutes, to monitor:

- order/merit marks;
- referrals: positive/negative;
- detentions;
- issues arising from checking registers – attendance/lates, etc.;
- behaviour issues – specific students;
- progress of specific students in reference to their targets (this information should be provided on a weekly basis by the tutors prior to your session together);
- meeting fortnightly with your line manager to help the pastoral co-ordinator gain an overview of what is happening in your year group and to discuss strategies for groups or individuals;
- regular meetings with the education welfare officer (EWO);
- supervising and directing the report card system in use in the school;
- monitoring IEPs and checking that they are used and regularly reviewed;
- involvement in referral meetings;
- monitoring registrations – ensuring that registers are taken every session and that they are marked correctly;

- seeing individual pupils and holding year detentions as necessary;
- responsibility for pupil progress by directing and co-ordinating initiatives for raising pupil attainment, including target setting for the pupils in your year group, in liaison with subject departments.

4 Developing year-group activities or events, including the PSHE programme

You are responsible for directing and co-ordinating activities which contribute to the personal, spiritual, moral, social and cultural development of the pupils within your year group.

Together with your tutor team you are responsible for developing and delivering:

- the PSHE programme and bank of PSHE materials;
- year-group assemblies;
- specific year-group events and activities, as decided (e.g. charity events, participation in drama competition, sports day, etc.);
- specific year-group sessions for pupils and parents (e.g. Y7 induction day, Y9 and Y11 option-choice evenings).

5 Liaison, communication and recording information

- organize pupil progress meetings for your year group;
- arrange meetings with individual parents to discuss welfare and general problems arising with any particular student;
- liaise closely with other schools as necessary (e.g. when new pupils enter the school or pupils leave the school);
- liaise with and meet the EWO and other outside agencies as necessary in respect of your year group;
- co-ordinate all information received from staff, parents and outside agencies regarding individual students, ensure that this information is distributed correctly and that any necessary actions are taken;
- direct the preparation of reports, records of achievement and references for your year group;
- liaise closely with subject departments in respect of the academic progress of individual pupils;
- collating and evaluating the data from panda (pupil performance information), teacher assessments, SATs, etc. via the assessment packages, and supporting form tutors in helping pupils to set targets;
- inform your line manager of any significant developments or major issues, which arise;
- keep clear and full records;
- year leaders should keep records/minutes of their team meetings;
- any letters/communications with pupils' homes, arrangements for parents meetings, etc. should go through the school office. Make sure that you give sufficient time for

the office to do all that you require. Copies should be provided for form tutors and placed on student files. It is your responsibility to check that two copies are made available to the parents on the list to receive additional copies of information regarding their child;

- referral and other monitoring forms should be kept in student files.

This role description may be renegotiated in the light of changes in staffing and the school development plan.

USING THE BIBLIOGRAPHY

This chapter is intended as an introduction to management. It is not meant to be definitive. You will find a bibliography and list of further reading at the end of each chapter so that, if you wish to do so, you can follow up topics. I have arranged it in this way so that you can see which books are relevant to particular themes.

BIBLIOGRAPHY AND FURTHER READING

Adair, J. (1988) *Effective Leadership*, London: Pan Books.

Bush, T. and Westburnham, J. (eds) (1994) *The Principles of Educational Management*, Harlow: Longman.

Blandford, S. (1997) *Middle Management in Schools*, London: Pitman Publishing.

Bennis, W. (1985) 'Leadership in the twenty-first century', *Journal of Organisational Change Management* 2(1).

Bennis, W. and Nannus, B. (1985) *Leaders: The Strategies for Taking Charge*, New York: Harper and Row.

Everard, K. B. (1986) *Developing Management in Schools*, Oxford: Basil Blackwell.

Everard, K. B. and Morris, G. (1985) *Effective School Management*, London: Harper & Row.

Everard, K. B. and Morris, G. (1990) *Effective School Management*, London: Paul Chapman Publishing.

Fullan, M. and Heargreaves, A. (1992) *What's Worth Fighting for in Your School?*, Buckingham: Open University Press.

Handy, C. (1993) *Understanding Organisations*, 4th edn, Harmondsworth: Penguin.

Handy, C. and Aiken, R. (1986) *Understanding Schools as Organisations*, Harmondsworth: Penguin.

Holmes, G. (1993) *Essential School Leadership*, London: Kogan Page.

Industrial Society, The (1985) *Management in Schools and Colleges Pack*, London: Industrial Society Press.

Peters, T. and Waterman, R. (1982) *In Search of Excellence*, London: Harper & Row.

Tannenbaum, R. and Schmidt, W. H. (1973) 'How to choose a leadership pattern', *Harvard Business Review* 36(2).

Chapter 2

What style of manager are you?

This chapter looks at some of the elements which make up management style. Figure 2.1 which shows the continuum of leadership behaviour, developed by Tannenbaum and Schmidt (1973), provides a useful way of considering this issue.

You will notice that the continuum moves from authoritarian, some versions say dictator, right the way across the possibilities until you reach laissez-faire (let be) or abdicator, in which you avoid carrying out your leadership responsibilities altogether. It describes a manager's working style in terms of *tells*, *sells*, etc, and the team's freedom in terms which vary from receiving instructions to having ownership of a problem.

Often I am asked: '*What is the best management style?*' I have to answer that there is no perfect management style. There are, however, fashions in management style. In the past when school leadership was much more dominated by very strong heads, who held almost absolute power, authoritarian leadership was in vogue, but of course there was little scope for real middle managers in this set-up. More recently, it is generally considered that effective managers involve and consult their teams whenever possible, though how truly democratic they are varies.

What is clear is that each individual will have a dominant or natural style. Case studies 2.1 and 2.2 point to a stark contrast in working styles.

CASE STUDY 2.1

Mr Shaw

Mr Shaw sees us once a fortnight. He uses his classroom for this after-school session, which is compulsory for us. He sits behind his desk to chair the meeting, while we sit facing him on hard-backed chairs as if we are pupils in his form. He briefs us on what has gone on in the last 14 days, and goes through with us what has to be done in the next fortnight. He is really giving us our orders. His instructions are clear and his paperwork is meticulous. We know precisely what is expected of us. Sometimes, but not always, we are told why an action is required. We are neither consulted about what we think, nor encouraged to make any suggestions. He is a good organizer and his plans work well, but there is never any discussion of the issue and he takes all the decisions himself. He is not a developmental manager. In fact, if anyone is unwise enough to make a suggestion, s/he will be quite sharply put down.

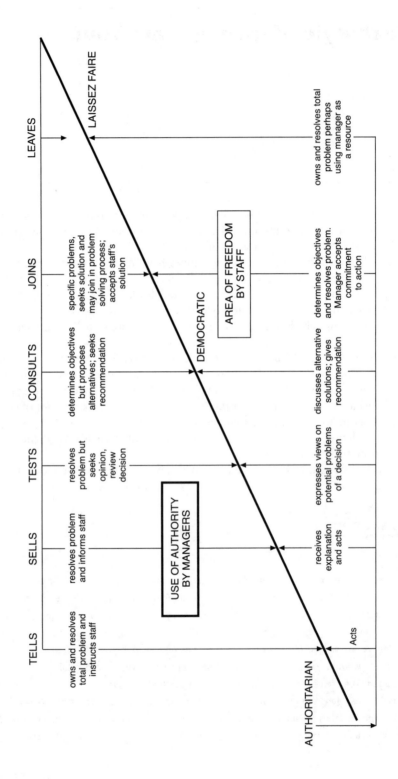

Figure 2.1 Continuum of leadership behaviour.

In this extract a tutor is describing her year leader's management style. The manager's style is authoritarian. He is strong on control and concentrates on managing the task. He knows precisely what he wants the team to do, and how much they have to know in order to do it. He is, however, weak on interacting with people. They are told what to do and expected to follow instructions. In this case there is some trust because they know from past experience that his schemes are well planned and tend to work, but the tutor comments regretfully, '*Mr Shaw is not a developmental manager ...*' This leader does not trust his team sufficiently to allow individual members to take any real responsibility.

Compare Mr Shaw with Mrs Lea.

CASE STUDY 2.2

Mrs Lea

We discuss everything. It takes time, but we really feel involved. We not only know what is going on, but are all involved in making the decisions, which are corporate. Occasionally Mrs Lea is not on top of the paperwork, but we understand this because of the time that she spends dealing with all the personal problems in the year group. Not only does she give very freely of her time to the pupils, but she is also interested in us both as a team and as individuals. She always makes time to listen and we particularly appreciate the quality of support that she gives to us.

Mrs Lea is not only democratic, she is also people orientated. In this short extract, the member of her team comments that this team feels involved, consulted and motivated. She has given them ownership of the problems, but supports them as a group and as individuals. She is not, however, always on top of the 'paperwork'. The team member, who clearly approves of her manager's style, feels that this is a price worth paying; nevertheless, administration is not this manager's forte.

Notice that what makes the difference in the two examples is how these managers treat the people in the team. Mr Shaw is only interested in directing and instructing his team. He has no interest in their views or perceptions of the issues. Mrs Lea is interested in them both as members of the team and individually. This team takes decisions corporately. The work priorities of the two managers are also clearly different. Mr Shaw's priority is the pastoral tasks that must be carried out in the next 2 weeks, a lot of which will be administrative, absence returns, etc. Mrs Lea's concentration on the people doesn't mean that she does not have objectives, but that they are formulated by the team working together. However, her lowest priority is dealing with the paperwork. At one time management 'gurus' disagreed as to whether good managers should be task or people orientated. Now it is generally agreed that to be an effective manager, you have to be able to cope with both aspects of the role. As you are likely naturally to be better at one than the other, you may find that you need some training in the less well-developed area in order to improve your skill.

THE MCGREGOR AXIS

Douglas McGregor first outlined his theory in *The Human Side of Management* (McGregor 1960) and developed it in *Leadership and Motivation* (McGregor 1966). He defined a model of management style – Theory X and Theory Y. McGregor set his ideas out on an axis as shown in Figure 2.2. The axis is based on your assumptions about people's likely behaviour, which in turn is a key factor in the level of motivation that you are likely to produce in the people in your team.

We all know that if a manager takes a McGregor X view of us this can have a depressing effect on our motivation and self-esteem. When applied to middle management in schools, a Theory X manager will be less committed to a team approach. Authoritarian managers tend to be McGregor X. They make such statements as:

> *People won't understand it, you know ...*
> *I can't trust people to do what I want them ...*
> *... It won't work because there are always some people, who won't do it properly ...*

Laissez-faire managers are usually but not always McGregor Y. They make such statements as:

> *I can rely on my team ...*
> *If I leave them to get on with it, they will do the job/task as well as I could ...*

McGregor X	McGregor Y
Manager assumes	Manager assumes
People don't naturally want to work	People react according to the conditions. Work can be a satisfier or a punishment
People are not naturally motivated	People are innately motivated and want to do well
People are not interested in improving their performance	People are always interested in improving their performance
People need close supervision. They have to be coerced, controlled and directed	Under the right conditions, people can be self-starters, and work effectively towards objectives, to which they are committed
Most people, have little ambition, avoid responsibility and actively want security	People learn not only to accept responsibility, but also seek responsibility.

Figure 2.2 Managerial assumptions.

The job gets done, doesn't it?
I leave it to so-and-so, you should have a word with her ...

A McGregor Y view of us may well improve our motivation provided that the conditions exist for us to develop our skills and perform. McGregor found that, in many situations, managers who used Theory Y assumptions did achieve better results. This also led him to the belief that many more people are able to contribute creatively to the solution of organizational problems than actually do so.

This does not mean that the solution to all your problems is to try to become a laissez-faire manager. A negative laissez-faire manager becomes McGregor X. You will hear him/her say:

It's not worth bothering about, as nobody does what I ask them to do anyway ...
There's no one with any spark here, so I just let them get on with it ...

What is important is to get the balance right. Real motivation only comes when people are clear about what they should be doing. The extreme McGregor Y laissez-faire manager can be just as demotivating and frustrating to work with as a McGregor X authoritarian.

Your own natural tendency is only one of the factors that you should take into account when deciding your management style. The situation in which you find yourself, the needs and skills of the team and their previous experience can all affect how you manage the team. Case Study 4.2 describes a recently appointed year head, who has difficulty in taking over a team. She wants to be democratic and consult her team, but it was not used to this approach and took the view that she was not providing sufficient leadership. At the beginning an over-democratic approach may be inappropriate. You do not know the team and at this time you need to establish yourself as the leader. Both of these factors could make you more authoritarian than you may be naturally, or indeed will be at a later stage of the team's development, when you know each other better, and are more used to working together. When this happens you will be more willing to delegate responsibilities than at the beginning and the team members should be more willing to undertake them. It is difficult to work in a style which does not come naturally to you for any length of time. The transitional period, in which you modify your natural style and adopt a formal, authoritarian approach, should, however, only last a few months at the most.

The task itself may be more suited to one particular management style. No one will thank you for having a lengthy debate over something which does not warrant it and where it would be better to explain briefly what the situation is and give directions about what will have to be done. Similarly, however consultative you are, crises occur and, as the year leader, you will have to take some on-the-spot important decisions. Concern for a pupil's safety may sometimes over ride your desire to consult and inform colleagues. These situations are generally understood to be exceptions to your normal practice.

Brown and Rutherford (1996) provide a further insight into roles which middle managers might take in schools. Some of these might well apply to a pastoral leader:

- *servant leader* – serving pupils, teachers and senior management. Fiona, in Case Study 1.1, may have perceived herself as a servant leader;
- *organizational architect* – engaging in professional discussions;
- *moral educator* – committed to high educational values;
- *social architect* – sensitive to the needs of pupils and staff. This role is frequently assumed by pastoral leaders;
- *leading professional* – spending the majority of his/her time teaching, leading the team comes second. Subject leaders are more likely to take on this role than pastoral leaders who usually feel guilty about not doing enough for their subject responsibility however much time they devote to it.

OMEGA MANAGERS

This is a concept developed by Neil Miller. He divides managers into four broad categories. Two of these we have come across already – the *authoritarian* and the *do nothing* (laissez-faire). The third category he describes as '*country club*'. Country-club managers are people orientated and run happy teams, but these teams sometimes underachieve in terms of the tasks that they have to perform. The fourth category Miller terms the omega managers. Omega is the last letter of the ancient Greek alphabet and means 'all things'. This does not mean that the omega manager is all things to all people, rather that s/he manages to combine effectively managing both tasks and people. Unlike Mrs Lea, described in Case Study 2.2, the omega manager successfully finds time for all the people who require help or support, without failing to complete his/her administrative task.

WHAT CHARACTERIZES THE OMEGA MANAGER?

These are some of the things that people who work with omega managers say about their team or their team leader.
  About the team:

- *this team has really high standards;*
- *we all know and agree about what we are trying to do ...;*
- *it is good to have clear objectives. It helps you concentrate on what is really important;*
- *when we have meetings, everyone gets a say and everyone is listened to ...;*
- *it's good to be able to rely on other people;*
- *I know that if a deadline is set, we'll meet it, and that no one will come to me on the last day and change the goal posts;*
- *we don't always agree on things, but we respect each other's views. What I like is that we can discuss an issue and disagree without descending to personalities;*
- *I like the way that we evaluate each thing that we do. We don't spend too much*

time, but always make time to ask: Did it go well, and what co
next time?

About the team leader:

- *she works hard and expects the same from us;*
- *he really does listen to what we have to say;*
- *she notices what we do and always thanks you or comments;*
- *she can criticise constructively and I learn from what she says. It's never personal;*
- *he is firm but fair;*
- *if he doesn't like something, he tells me, not the world;*
- *she is not afraid to make difficult decisions;*
- *there is no doubt about who is leader of this team, but we are all made to feel that we are contributing.*

FOR REFLECTION

Weindling and Earley (1987) undertook research for the NFER (National Foundation for Educational Research) into how new head teachers prepared themselves for their role and managed their schools during the first year of their headship. When assessing how these new head teachers perceived themselves and how they were perceived, a clear discrepancy emerged. Almost all the new head teachers perceived themselves as consultative and democratic. In most cases, however, their staff did not agree. The teachers and support staff viewed the head teachers as far more 'tells or sells' than consults. It could therefore be useful for you to find out how your team perceives you and what they think your dominant management style is.

CASE STUDY 2.3

For reflection

In Chapter 1, we considered the case of Fiona, a new manager, who did not understand her role and made a lot of mistakes because she had no concept of what it meant to be a leader. Throughout Chapters 1 and 2, I stressed that there is no blueprint for effectiveness as a manager, but it seems unfair not to offer you any guidelines for success. It also seems appropriate to end this section by giving Fiona some concise tips on how to lead her team. For this purpose, I am quoting from Fullan and Hargreaves (1992) with some slight modifications.

Key points for leaders to remember

1. *Keep it simple and clear* – always remember the danger of overplanning and over-management.
2. *Avoid 'if-only' statements* – transferring the blame for actions 'beyond your control' renders people powerless and inactive. It can also make them resentful.
3. *Distinguish the wood from its trees and concentrate on the important issues* – for example: be clear what are your aims for your year group and how you are going to achieve them.
4. *Practice being brave* – if the leader takes risks, staff are more likely to be innovative, strong-minded and clearly focused. Choose your risks carefully – don't be foolhardy!
5. *Empower others* – staff need room and permission to try things out. They also need celebrating occasions for success.
6. *Build visions* – remember it is not only you who needs to have a vision. Share the vision and enable others to participate in developing the vision. Encourage team members to have ideas, which they can contribute.
7. *Decide what not to do* – time management. Doing things right, but doing the right things.
8. *Find some allies* – interdependence is crucial for the stimulation of intellectual curiosity and the sharing of ideas. If you do not find allies, it is very difficult to succeed in the initiatives you want to run.
9. *To sum up* – remember that a good leader is never a one-person band. S/he keeps his/her followers, supports, motivates, encourages and develops them, and knows when to encourage them to seek leadership positions themselves.

BIBLIOGRAPHY AND FURTHER READING

Brown, M. and Rutherford, D. (1996) *Leadership For School Improvement, The Changing Role of the Head of Department*, Cambridge: BEMAS Partners in Change Conference.

Fullan, M. and Hargreaves, A. (1992) *What's Worth Fighting for in Your School*, Buckingham: Open University Press.

McGregor, D. (1960) *The Human Side of Management*, McGraw-Hill.

McGregor, D. (1966) *Leadership and Motivation*, MIT Press.

Tannenbaum, R. and Schmidt, W. H. (1973) 'How to choose a leadership pattern', *Harvard Business Review* 36(2).

Weindling, D. and Earley, P. (1987) *Secondary Headship, the First Years*, Windsor: National Foundation for education research, NFER/Nelson.

Chapter 3

Effective administration

I just didn't realize how much administration there would be. I thought that I would be spending most of my time dealing with pupils and their problems, but actually I have to spend an enormous amount of time processing information and dealing with the paperwork. The sheer volume of it gets to me and depresses me. I never feel that I am on top of it. In fact I have to run fast to stand still, and I feel that, as an administrator, I am reactive rather than proactive ...

An experienced year head attending a course on improving his management skills made this comment. It sums up one of the main problems faced by pastoral managers. The administrative workload is extremely heavy, a lot of it comes down to you, either from the senior management or from outside agencies, so it is reactive, and there is always an urgency factor – you have to do it now, if not sooner!

The time available to a middle manager in a school to deal with the administrative tasks in school time is necessarily limited by your teaching commitment. This applies to both pastoral and subject leaders, but in your case the problem is compounded by the crises, which occur on a daily basis, and for which you cannot plan. Some crises are so serious that they interrupt your teaching. Schools vary in what attitude they take to a year head seeking cover because s/he has to abandon a lesson in order to deal with pupil problems. My advice would be only to seek cover for a real emergency, otherwise you attract a reputation as someone who finds excuses to avoid his/her teaching commitment and other staff and the pupils will not like this at all, but this is not the main issue here. Your real problem is how to use your 'free' time effectively. However good a time manager you are, there is no way that you can expect to safeguard a particular free period for your lesson marking or to work on administration, as you simply cannot know when major problems will arise.

The administration of your house or year group and the paperwork which goes with it are important parts of your management responsibility, but they are the means to an end, not the end itself. Nevertheless if you don't manage them well, they can limit your effectiveness in dealing with the real issues. The small amount of time available for this aspect of your job means that you have to have the procedures in place to help you do the tasks well. You also have to ensure that where you are reliant on information and returns supplied by others, it is straightforward and easy for them to complete. Being an efficient administrator is one of the keys to success as a middle manager. Being a good manager of time helps you achieve your aim of running your section efficiently. The two skills are linked closely together and, on the courses I run, more people tell me that they want to improve their time-management skills than any other single area of management expertise.

Properly defined routines for all potentially time-consuming activities are a crucial success factor. When you take up a new post be prepared to spend time on creating procedures that work, because this will pay dividends later on when you are pushed and need to deal with administration virtually on autopilot. Well-thought-out procedures and effective systems not only contribute to the section's efficiency and to your reputation as a sound administrator, but will also strengthen the sense of working together and release staff energies and time for tackling the very many other tasks that await.

Teachers have always been critical of the sheer volume of paperwork with which they have to deal, and claimed that they should be free to concentrate on teaching. The number of administrative tasks needing to be done and the volume of paperwork has certainly not decreased over time, although the nature of some of it has changed, and more of it now has to be computerized than in the past. Indeed, teachers have never been under so much pressure to manage efficiently as they are today. If the paperwork is not well managed, it can easily become a burden and erode time that should be free for you to do other more interesting jobs, or, better still, to relax. You can, however, help yourself by creating clear and time-effective systems.

WHAT ARE THE MAIN ADMINISTRATIVE TASKS?

Administration is more than just paperwork. Your administrative tasks will fall mainly into three categories:

1 Managing the day-to-day tasks associated with your team's normal work

For example:

- checking registers and following up absences;
- collecting and collating information about pupils or pastoral issues;
- producing reports on pupils for the senior management team (SMT) or education welfare officers (EWOs)/social workers;
- responding to requests for information, communicating with or feeding back to the members of the team or to parents.

2 Organizing and administering the year's contribution to occasional school events and activities

For example:

- sports day;
- pupil-progress evenings for parents;
- parents sessions (e.g. on aspects of the Personal, Social and Health Education [PSHE] curriculum).

3 Dealing with all the paper which finds its way into your pigeon-hole or onto your desk

An exercise to focus your thinking about handling the paperwork can be found later in this chapter.

To be a good administrator you have to manage time, resources, communication and people effectively.

First identify the potential time-wasters and try to avoid them. The worst major time-wasters fall into five main categories:

- poor organization;
- poor planning;
- paperwork;
- meetings;
- interruptions.

Poor organization

Examples include:

- not having everything you need to do a task to hand at the time when you have to do the job;
- your inaccuracy and inattention to detail causes other people to have to spend time putting the situation right – this could make you extremely unpopular.

Coping with your administrative responsibility means organizing yourself and others efficiently.

Poor planning

This could include:

- because you haven't planned ahead sufficiently well you find yourself having to concentrate on very important tasks when you are worn out;
- too many meetings or a clash on the same day;
- finding that you have to undertake an important activity on the spur of the moment.

Planning ahead is extremely important.

Paperwork

This could include:

- your desk is so full of paper that you can't find anything;
- having no system for dealing with the paperwork or having a poor filing system;
- finding yourself regularly handling paperwork which is not relevant to your job.

Dealing with your paperwork is discussed fully below.

Meetings

Meetings are often cited as a major time-waster. This is because:

- poorly prepared meetings take a long time and tend to achieve very little;
- poorly focused meetings neither provide adequate information nor allow issues to be discussed properly – they waste time;
- badly led meetings drag on;
- team members come with their own baggage and highjack the meeting.

Interruptions

Interruptions stop you getting on with the work you want to do. Examples include:

- pupils who need to see you;
- colleagues who want a word;
- parents who arrive without an appointment;
- events arranged at inconvenient times – fire drill is an obvious example;
- advisors, governors, etc. who happen to have popped in and visit you, etc.

You cannot afford to waste valuable time. Even identifying the potential time-wasters can help you afford falling into some of these traps. Advice about how to deal with most of these problems will be given in the ten points itemized in the next section.

HOW TO BE AN EFFECTIVE ADMINISTRATOR

Ten pointers:

1. plan ahead;
2. prioritize;
3. action plan;
4. make the time that you need;
5. discipline your decision making;
6. communicate;
7. avoid stress and learn to say 'No';
8. delegate;
9. don't clutter up your spaces;
10. create an efficient filing system.

This list is adapted from: Kemp R. and Nathan M. (1995).

Plan ahead – identify long-term goals, make middle-term plans and plan the day

If you organize your time well, identify the long-term goals, plan ahead and create clear routines, you can avoid falling into last-minute crisis management. A lot of your work (e.g. following up absences or meeting the EWO) comes on a weekly cycle and can be programmed in as a regular activity. You will have a pro forma for absences that you can issue weekly, probably by putting them into pigeon-holes when you arrive on Monday morning, or by giving each tutor a term's supply at the beginning of each term. The tutors need to know that they must return the list of the week's absences to your pigeon-hole by lunchtime on Friday and that you will be seriously displeased if you do not receive it on time.

Similarly, you know when the progress meetings or major events, which will take up a lot of time, are to occur so you can plan ahead. A year planner can be a useful aid here, as it shows you when the very busy times will be. Work out a timetable and see how much of the planning and organization you can do well ahead of the event. You may want to use a flow chart, or the calendar section on your word-processing package. Word processing the calendar of events means that you can print it out and keep it clearly on the wall of your office (if you are lucky enough to have one) and amend it easily if, as often happens, events are added after the beginning of the school year. Keep copies of all the planning sheets, so that the second time around it is much easier for you. Another piece of advice for the first time is not to feel shy about asking an efficient year head how s/he does things. Adopting a good system will help you become effective yourself.

Prioritize

An effective manager always has a clear idea about the priorities for his or her work. For most of us, there always seems to be a mountain of things that need to be done. When you face such a mountain, ask yourself:

- *What are the important things?*
- *What are the urgent things?*

Some things will have a very high priority because they are so urgent, however, they may not actually be very important at all. This could mean that they could be done quickly without taking up too much time. Other things may have a high priority because they are extremely important. Some important tasks may not have an urgent deadline, but need a lot of thought. To do them properly and without a last-minute crisis, you have to make enough time for them when you plan out your work. This means accepting the fact that these kinds of thing can rarely be done in school time and that to hope to do them in school could put you on a route for disaster. They will occupy your evenings, so it is worth planning ahead to know when you can fit them in. Last-minuters may produce good work, but are rarely popular with their own department or with the management. Making clear middle- and long-term plans and prioritizing could help you to work better within the

	URGENT		IMPORTANT
Today:		1.	
This week:		2.	
		3.	
	NEITHER		URGENT & IMPORTANT

Figure 3.1 List of priorities.

deadlines. Examples of development plans are shown in Chapter 11 (p. 177). Notice that they include calculations of the time needed for the various stages.

Create a list of priorities and put them in order, so that you are clear what matters most. Filling them onto a chart like the one shown in Figure 3.1 could help you to see clearly what really matters and what needs to be done today or this week.

Action plan

Once you are clear about your priorities, it is useful to plan when you are going to do things. Time is always short, so make an action plan. For most people a week is the most convenient time-span for action planning and a year head needs to know what the week ahead holds for him/her. If and when additional tasks come your way during the week, determine their priority in relation to what you have already planned to do, and, when necessary, adjust your action plan accordingly. Have a copy of your weekly plan at home with you and one posted in school, so that when a crisis occurs you can see immediately the knock-on effect on your week. An exemplar of a weekly planning sheet may be found in Case Study 3.1. It is set out to show what a week could look like at the beginning of the week. The test is to prevent it from getting over full as the week progresses. Remember: do high-priority jobs well within the deadline, so that the tasks, which have to go by the board, will not be those that you really care about.

Make the time that you need

One of the difficulties in being a middle manager in a school is that your management tasks have to be fitted around the time you spend teaching. As I pointed out earlier in this chapter, this is compounded for a pastoral manager, because you have so little free time in school and it tends to be taken up in dealing with crises. This puts a premium on using the time that you have effectively. It also makes it important to develop a personal sense of time – otherwise you become reactive, simply spending your time doing the things that you are asked or told to do, rather than the things that you really want to do. An example of a personal planner, which allows you to distinguish between tasks that you must do and those that you would like to do, is included at the end of this chapter (p. 42). Your weekly planning sheet is an essential aid in structuring how you use the time available to best advantage. Try, for example, to make a regular slot for dealing with routine matters, such as 30 minutes at the start of the day before the pupils arrive with their problems.

It also means that you must be realistic about the time needed to do a job well. Experience in the post will help you to develop this essential skill, so that you allow enough time to do the important jobs properly. You will do them less well if you rush them or keep breaking off to do other things. If necessary set yourself a time limit for jobs that should not take long or which have a lower priority rating, and ensure that you free up enough time for the jobs which require thorough analysis before taking decisions. Sometimes attempting less and really concentrating on top priorities can increase your productivity and effectiveness.

Disciplining yourself to use every minute of time available is also a skill, which you develop over time, and out of necessity. '*I can never do any real work in school time . . .*' is a comment that I have often heard. '*Nonsense!*' is the short answer! It is a matter of choice. If you do not do any administrative work in school, you will have to take it all home and do it all in the evenings and this could put you onto a progressive spiral of tiredness. It is also neither an effective or professional use of your time. You will have to learn to distinguish between time spent gossiping and conversations in the staffroom which further your knowledge of a pupil or a problem. Although you do need some time to relax and will have to do the major thinking at home, my advice is to get on with the smaller, more mechanical tasks at school. Although you cannot rely on having the time on a regular basis, crises do not occur all the time – just when you least want them, so seize any moments you can to get the straightforward tasks completed. Case Study 3.3 will help you practise this skill.

Discipline your decision making

You will find that you will be deluged with information on a daily basis. Bits of paper of various sorts will constantly make its way to your pigeon-hole or desk. Your aim should be to handle each piece of paper *only once*. Make a decision on every bit of paper that crosses your desk or enters your pigeon-hole, even if it is only a decision to seek advice or to decide when you can take action. This may be easier said than done, but try to discipline yourself to take action on a piece of paper the first time it comes into your hands. Applying the principle of urgency and importance may also help.

Do not put off to tomorrow what you can do today. The first Duke of Wellington had a dictum that you should always do the business of the day in the day. This remains sound advice, especially in the light of the evidence that the average manager delays action on the majority of all the daily in-tray items that could have been disposed of at first handling. You may want to look again at the Industrial Society findings shown in Case Study 3.2.

Communicate

Good communications are vital for effective management. Information and decisions must be passed quickly and efficiently to the people who need to know both within your team and outside it.

When managers are appraised, communication is an area which tends to attract criticism. This is because we do not always communicate as clearly as we think we do, and because people do not listen or they hear what they want to hear. How you choose to communicate is up to you. Within your team you can use memos, a regular department bulletin, tell people personally or, most likely, a mixture of approaches. The only test is: Do the people who need to know actually know everything necessary to do the job properly?

Avoid stress and learn to say, 'No'

A lot of us find it very difficult to say 'No', when we are asked to do something, and if we do refuse we feel guilty even if the request is patently unreasonable. Yet if you take on too much, it will affect your overall performance and you could end up doing all the jobs badly, as well as becoming stressed out. This means that you have to make some difficult choices and adhere to the key idea of determining your priorities.

Here are four steps that you can use when saying 'No'

1. *Listen.* Listen carefully to make sure that you understand clearly what the request entails. This way you have also extended to the other person the courtesy of a proper hearing.
2. *Say 'No.'* This means really and clearly saying '*No*', not '*Maybe*', or '*I'm not sure*' or '*perhaps*', or '*I'll let you know tomorrow*'. Any of these will leave the requester with the hope that in the end you will do the quite unreasonable thing s/he has asked. Make sure that you sound firm, but not truculent or aggressive.
3. *Give your reason.* Always state your reason or reasons clearly, so that the other person knows why you have decided not to say 'Yes' to the request.
4. *Suggest alternatives.* If you can, suggest other ways the person might be able to tackle the task. This shows that you have thought about the problem.

Delegate

> *Without successful delegation, successful management is impossible...*
> Gloucestershire LEA advice to new heads of department

As the team leader, you are responsible for the smooth running of the year group and that means making sure that all the necessary tasks are done, not doing them all yourself.

In terms of how you organize and administer the work of your section, you are making a rod for your own back if you do try to do everything yourself. The advice normally given to managers is to try to delegate every task that you can. Even if you succeed, there will be plenty left for you. If you delegate effectively, you will have more time for the jobs that only you can do.

Don't clutter up your spaces

Do these scenarios describe you?

1. You are sure that the vital piece of paper is there somewhere, it is just that you can't lay your hand on it immediately because your desk or workspace is too cluttered to find things easily.
2. You go to the headteacher to request a new filing cabinet and find her signally unsympathetic. She suggests that rather than buy you a new filing cabinet, which would only occupy a lot of space in a very small year-head's office, you should clear out your existing cabinet regularly and get into the habit of throwing some things away.

It is never easy to keep your workspaces clear, especially if, as is the case for most year heads, you do not have much working space in the first place, nevertheless it is important to try. Your aim should be to try to have on your desk in front of you only what you are currently working on. Not only does the cluttered desk or overfull messy filing cabinet waste time, and fail to inspire confidence in your management systems, it is also usually evidence of poor decision making.

Create an efficient filing system

A lot of items fail to get filed, and so join the clutter on top of the desk because you cannot decide where to file them or how to label them.

The sort of filing system you develop is up to you – it will depend a lot on the facilities available in your school. Whatever the system, unless it is efficiently organized, you cannot hope to discipline your decision making and streamline your administrative work. Decide how you will categorize things and make your chosen system as clear and simple as possible, and then stick to it. If other members of the team have to use the filing cabinet, make sure that the system is user-friendly and understood by all. The time spent ensuring that others can operate the system easily will pay enormous dividends in terms of goodwill and co-operation.

Two tests of an effective filing system are:

1. Can you find anything you need in seconds rather than minutes?
2. Can you quickly explain where to find, e.g. an item for PSHE, to someone else in the team, and can they then locate it easily?

I deliver middle-management seminars for pastoral leaders in cities throughout Britain, and have been shown numerous examples of good practice. What has impressed me most is that most of the monitoring mechanisms do not occupy a lot of space in filing cabinets, but are concise and easily accessible. Often information for a whole year group over a period of time has been reduced to one sheet of A4. The weekly or monthly absence figures for the classes in the year group is an example of this. The use of the optical mark reader has made it easier to monitor absence or punctuality than in the past. Using the sheet, the year tutor can gain a clear picture of absence over the week or month in each class, make comparisons between tutor groups or monitor a particular group. They can be kept in a file for the year or added to a spreadsheet.

The headteacher was not being unsympathetic when she said, 'Get into the habit of throwing away what you do not need or will never use again'. It is all too tempting to keep things because they might be useful someday. A regular review and purge of the contents of your filing cabinet, particularly of items that have not been used for ages, or that are out of date, makes a lot of sense.

CASE STUDY 3.1

A weekly planning sheet – Exemplar

This is what the head of year 10's weekly planner looked like at the beginning of the week:

	1	2	3	Lunch	4	5	AS
Monday before school: distribute agenda for year team meeting (remind them that AOB should be in before the meeting)			Free – Mrs Barnes – mother of Victoria	Subject meeting – assessments Y10			Supervise Homework Club
Tuesday	Free – see HT – regular monthly meeting (re. year group)			Year surgery			Supervise year detention
Wednesday Duty day					Free		Bus duty
Thursday Year assembly: check that tutors are on target for getting sets of reports to you for Friday	Free						Year team meeting. Check reports again. Take home any completed set and start checking them
Friday Before school: see Mr Plant, father of Norman		Free Continue to chase and collect the sets of reports for signing. Follow up from meeting				Free	Set that all the sets of reports are in for signing
Weekend	Check and sign half-year reports						

1 INDUSTRIAL SOCIETY FINDINGS

- *20 per cent of management time is wasted* (i.e. 1 day per week) – a huge waste of expensive resources;
- *90 per cent of directors/managers work with a cluttered desk* (the cost is an average 35 minutes per day looking for paper);
- *17 per cent of senior management time is spent in internal meetings* (badly organized and chaired meetings are a major time-waster);
- *26–33 per cent of managers' time is spent on paperwork* (could this be reduced with more effective systems?);
- *78 per cent of managers do not work whilst travelling* (so 12–14 per cent of the working week is totally ineffective).

For reflection

Think about these findings in the context of your own school.

2 PROCRASTINATION

Originally reproduced from MacKensie (1979).

- Schedule the difficult – the important – the unpleasant tasks first. Then follow your schedule.
- Set deadlines and 'go public' by announcing them.
- Set acceptable standards, but avoid perfectionism. Perfection is unobtainable.
- Handle a job just once. When you pick it up, dispose of it.
- Develop a philosophy about mistakes that will help you learn from them.
- Reward yourself after the job is done.

Remember: the average manager delays action on 60 per cent of those in-tray items which could have been disposed of on first handling.

For reflection

How could your own practice benefit from applying these guidelines?

Identify the potential time-wasters and try to avoid them. The worst major time-wasters fall into five main categories:

- poor planning;
- poor organization;

- paperwork;
- meetings;
- interruptions.

You cannot afford to waste valuable time. Even identifying the potential time-wasters can help you afford falling into some of these traps. Advice about how to deal with most of these problems will be given in the ten points given in Case Study 3.4.

CASE STUDY 3.3

For action

This case study allows you to practise your time-management skills, and apply the ideas suggested above, either individually or as a group of year heads. It follows through a typical year head's day, starting with the expected timetable. Your task is to try to deal with all the jobs and problems described in the scenario. You will also find some questions to answer. Remember that in real life you will not know what happens next.

Although the day described may not match the schedule used in your own school, what you are actually trying to establish is what principles should you use to tackle the problems most effectively. The day, which only takes you up to break, is no worse than many year heads regularly have to face. This is deliberate because you need a typical day to focus your thinking, not an especially difficult one. The year head whose day is described here is clearly not yet a perfect manager of time as there are one or two items that a good time manager would not have left to do on the day.

Managing your time effectively

Time is your most important resource – be ruthless in your defence of it!

A year head's day – I

You have just arrived at school. It is 8.15. This is what your programme for the day looks like:

- 8.30–8.40   Go through your post and items in your pigeon-hole
- 8.40–8.50   Head's daily briefing for staff
- 8.50–9.00   Check that all the registers in your year group are covered
                Take a register if necessary
- 9.00   Take your year assembly in the small hall
- 9.10–9.50   Lesson 1: teach Year 8
- 9.50–10.30   Lesson 2: teach Year 9
- 10.30–10.50   Break
- 10.50–11.30   Lesson 3: free period
- 11.30–12.10   Lesson 4: free period – meeting with a parent scheduled
- 12.10–1.10   Lunch

- 1.10–1.20   Afternoon registration; check that all registers are covered
- 1.20–2.00   Lesson 5: teach Year 12, 'A' Level
- 2.00–2.40   Lesson 6: teach Year 12, 'A' Level
- 2.40–3.00   Lesson 7: teach Year 10
- 3.00–3.40   Lesson 8: teach Year 10
- 3.40–3.50   Coach duty
- 3.50–5.00   Year heads' meeting.

In your free period for the day you hope to: finalize the presentation that you have to make to the year heads' meeting tonight (the head is going to attend this meeting), check that the overhead projector is available and working and finish marking Year 10's books. You teach Year 10 this afternoon and have promised to have them marked.

A year head's day – 2 (dealing with your paperwork)

This is what you found in your pigeon-hole when you arrived at school. You have 30 minutes before the start of the day to try to do a first deal with this paperwork. Using the guidelines provided, decide what you should do with each of these bits of paper (*remember: your aim is to handle each bit of paper only once if possible*):

- three publishers' catalogues, some leaflets and several communications about relevant courses;
- an invitation to a meeting at the local Teachers' Centre about changes to Special Educational Needs (SEN) practice (reply date: Wednesday). You are not the Senco, but will need to know about changes to practice because you have to supply information according to regulations;
- a letter of complaint from a parent about an incident involving one of your tutors;
- a note from the school secretary – arrangements for a visiting PSHE speaker appear to have some problems, please see her to sort it out. The speaker is expected on Friday for an hour's session with the whole year group. In this school, your pastoral responsibility includes organizing PSHE for your year group;
- a note from the Bursar about payment for a new set of PSHE materials. The computer is claiming you are overspent. You don't think that you are overspent. She also says that other materials have arrived and are in her office – please will you collect them ASAP as they are taking up a lot of room;
- a curt note from your most difficult tutor saying that he wants to see you urgently about a very important matter. The note does not say what the problem is;
- a letter from a parent wanting an appointment about the progress of her son;
- a reminder from the EWO that your regular meetings seem to have gone by the board in the last few weeks and suggesting that you fix a date for her to come to see you;
- a letter offering places for a few of your year group to attend a conference – the places are allotted on a first-come-first-served basis;
- a short sharp note from the headteacher saying – I need to see you urgently about a problem.

Time and task management

A year head's day – 3 (urgency versus importance: some typical year-head problems)

It is 8.40 (5 minutes before morning registration) and these problems face you as Head of Year:

- two tutors seem not to have arrived yet;
- a child from your year group has arrived at the staffroom door in a fairly upset state. She is from one of the two tutor groups where the tutor hasn't arrived yet;
- the school secretary comes into the staffroom with a phone message from a parent. It's about a school trip tomorrow. Do the pupils have to wear school uniform and what time is the trip returning? If it is after the close of the school day her son would miss the school coach and would have difficulty getting home. The secretary says that the parent sounded rather agitated about things and would like to talk to you;
- a passing comment from a head of department seems to indicate that one of your form tutors is not following the procedures about following up pupil absences that you all agreed at the last Year meeting. The tutor is new to your team, and you have the gut feeling that this may be the tip of an iceberg.

For action

Put these problems in order of urgency:
- Which are the most important and why?
- What strategies should you adopt in dealing with them?

A year head's day – 4

At break you return to the staffroom. Your pigeon-hole has some more messages including this one, which is marked 'urgent':

Danny Jorge in my form tells me he has lost some money – about £20. He says that he had two £10 notes with him yesterday. Instead of handing it in to the Bursar, he kept it in his pocket, then at lunch time apparently he put it in his desk, and he thinks he forgot to put it back in his pocket in the afternoon. He didn't think about it again until he was on the train to go home. Even then he didn't come back to look for it, and this morning the money is missing. He can be careless as well as forgetful so there is the possibility that either he lost it or it simply fell out of his pocket, but it is definitely missing now. I tried to see you before assembly, but you seemed to be busy.

While you are reading this communication, a newly qualified teacher (NQT) arrives in a very upset state. She's on duty today and encountered a girls' fight in the playground. The girls paid absolutely no attention to her instruction to stop the fight. They seem to be tearing each other's hair out and their friends are loudly egging them on. You are the Year Head, so please will you help her!

For action

What action should you take to deal with these problems? How do they affect your timetable for the day?

CASE STUDY 3.4

For action/discussion

Top ten time thieves:

- telephone interruptions;
- people dropping in – usually with a problem;
- poor information between departments;
- problems with computers – 'technofailure';
- changed priorities caused by colleagues;
- lack of organizational planning;
- poor listening skills of others;
- inappropriate organization structure;
- moving goalposts;
- putting things right that were not wrong in the first place.

For discussion

1. Identifying the problems is the first step towards solving them. Do you agree that these are the main 'time thieves'? Change the list to describe the main problems that you face in your job.
2. Consider doing a time-log. Do not turn this into a burden. The idea is that you use it to assess how you use your time. For example ... what effect do the time thieves have on your working week? Are you spending too much time on the more trivial administrative tasks and not leaving enough for the strategic tasks?
3. What strategies do you use to steer clear of or deal with the problem of time thieves?

CASE STUDY 3.5

Exemplar – A way of organizing your tasks over a month or half a term

Must do			
What	By when	Time needed	Resources needed
1.			
2.			
3.			
4.			

Would like to do			
What	By when	Time needed	Resources needed
1.			
2.			
3.			
4.			

BIBLIOGRAPHY AND FURTHER READING

Kemp, R. and Nathan, M. (1989) *Middle Management in Schools, A Survival Guide*, Oxford: Basil Blackwell (reprinted by Stanley Thorne 1995).

MacKensie, R. A. (1979) *MacKensie on Time*, New York: Amacom.

Nelson, I. (1995) *Time Management for Teachers*, Professional skills for teachers series, London: Kogan Page.

Gloucestershire LEA *Advice to New Heads of Department*. Gloucestershire LEA.

British Gas *Time Management Unit for Heads of Science*, British Gas.

Chapter 4

Building and developing a pastoral team

What is a team?
A group in which the individuals have a common aim and in which the jobs and skills of each member fit with those of others, as in a jigsaw puzzle.

What is teamwork?
Groups become teams through disciplined action. They shape a common purpose, agree on performance, define a common working approach, develop high levels of complementary skills and hold themselves mutually accountable for results. And, as with any effective discipline, they never stop doing any of these things.

Katzenbach and Smith (1993)

SOME QUESTIONS FOR YOU TO THINK ABOUT

1. Why are teams important?
2. What are the stages of team formation?
3. What stage of development is your team at now?
4. How do you recognize an effective team?
5. What are the special features/problems of managing a pastoral team?
6. What are the roles that people play in teams?
7. What special problems/difficulties do members of year teams face?
8. How can you address these problems? Can you take a management approach?

This chapter will try to address the questions on the list above.

I   Why teams are important

In the past teachers were very much individualists, specialists in their own fields, but working in isolation behind the closed door of their own classroom. This attitude is no longer the norm and now it is generally agreed that people working together can achieve more than individuals working separately. This is true of a pastoral team as much as of a subject department. It is also true that you can achieve more from your team if you have a good understanding of how it works (Figure 4.1).

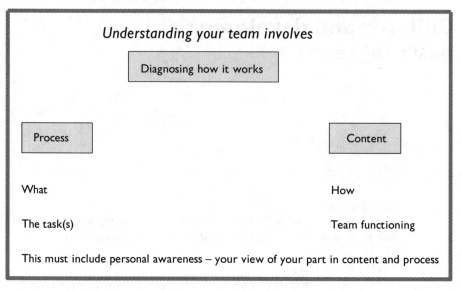

Figure 4.1 Understanding your team.

2 Stages of team formation

Building an effective team is not an overnight process – it takes time and effort. Some teams unite easily, others are very difficult indeed and a few never work effectively. Building a pastoral team has some special problems. An example of a pastoral team, containing some very difficult team members, may be found in Case Study 4.3. Team development typically displays four stages. The version used here was developed for the Industrial Society. I find it useful, and you should be able to use the model to help think about what state of development your own team is in.

Forming

This is the initial stage in which the team is put together. Commercial organizations use a whole battery of aptitude and personality tests to help them put together teams, which are likely to be effective. In a school, however, if you are a head of department or head of year, you are unlikely to enjoy the luxury of selecting your own team. Most likely you will take over an existing team and only over a period of time will you be able to replace some of the members.

Storming

This is the stage which is characterized by tensions as team members jockey for position, or the hostilities, which were initially repressed, come to the fore. There is likely to be mistrust of your actions or motives, the level of co-operation is likely to be low, proposed changes are likely to meet with opposition and your leadership may well be challenged. At this stage team-leader actions may well be dominated by 'telling' as you have to impose your authority or lose control and because the team members seem reluctant to contribute as they want you to prove yourself.

Norming or welding

This is the stage when the team begins to come together. Relations between you and some of the members may still be formal and disagreements and conflicts may remain hidden beneath the surface, yet progress is being made as tension decreases. Roles and positions are being sorted out and this enables you to delegate more to team members.

Performing

This is the operational target you are aiming for. This stage is characterized by a high level of trust and support among team members and by openness in discussion that is not achieved at other stages. Conflicts and disagreements can be brought into the open and discussed. The strengths of the team members are recognized and used by the team to achieve its objectives. The team is confident enough to be self-critical and accept and use outside advice.

Many teams go through all four stages in their building process, some never reach the latter stages and a fortunate few jump through the early stages quickly to reach full potential.

3   Analysing what stage of development your team is in

Think about the team of which you are the leader – which stage of development is it in now? Are you norming, storming, welding or performing? If you discussed the issue with the members of your team, would you expect them all to agree with your verdict of what stage the team is in?

Undertaking a pastoral team audit

Answering the following questions about the team should help identify those aspects of its responsibilities it feels it does well and those which need attention. You may wish to amend some of the questions to make them fit your particular team. This is not a problem as in this questionnaire there is no set number of questions.

How to do the audit

Circle the number which you feel most accurately reflects the current stage of development. Use the following scale:

1 = as good as you can get it;
2 = pleased with where we are at;
3 = satisfied;
4 = not very happy;
5 = unhappy and dissatisfied.

The team

Everyone is clear about his/her roles and responsibilities	1	2	3	4	5
Members of the team share ideas, materials and approaches	1	2	3	4	5
Individual skills are recognized and used effectively	1	2	3	4	5
New members of the team are supported and given appropriate induction	1	2	3	4	5
There is clarity about delegated decision making	1	2	3	4	5
Major decisions affecting the work of the team are made collectively	1	2	3	4	5
All members of the team feel able to ask questions and express opinions	1	2	3	4	5
The professional development needs of all members of the team are met	1	2	3	4	5
Individual professional development is shared with other team members	1	2	3	4	5

Relationships with parents and others

Good relationships between parents and the team members predominate	1	2	3	4	5
Parents are kept informed about their child's progress in an appropriate manner	1	2	3	4	5
The agreed procedures for parents' meetings or letters home are followed by all team members	1	2	3	4	5
Reports are informative and written in user-friendly language	1	2	3	4	5
Tutor comments are full and constructive	1	2	3	4	5
Tutors are kept informed about developments in cases concerning members of their tutor groups	1	2	3	4	5
Opportunities for tutors and parents to discuss pupil progress are provided and used effectively	1	2	3	4	5
Tutors are kept informed of changes in personnel or procedures (e.g. in the support agencies or SEN)	1	2	3	4	5

Pupils

Pupils and tutors treat each other with respect	1	2	3	4	5
Tutorial time is used effectively	1	2	3	4	5
A range of pupil achievement is recognized and celebrated	1	2	3	4	5
Feedback to pupils is regular and constructive	1	2	3	4	5
Pupils feel able to seek advice or support from the year head	1	2	3	4	5
Pupils feel able to turn to their tutor for support or advice	1	2	3	4	5
Pupils understand the standards of behaviour expected of them	1	2	3	4	5
Pupils demonstrate high standards of behaviour	1	2	3	4	5
Pupils are encouraged to collaborate and work together appropriately	1	2	3	4	5

Organizational

Team documents are in place (i.e. there are useful, manageable and up-to-date guidelines	1	2	3	4	5
Appropriate record forms are available for the tutors to use	1	2	3	4	5
Tutors use records to inform their interaction with pupils	1	2	3	4	5
Attendance is monitored and absences followed up	1	2	3	4	5
Punctuality is monitored and strategies for dealing with lateness are in place and used by team members	1	2	3	4	5
Information needed by the tutors is accessible	1	2	3	4	5
Registers comply with current legislation	1	2	3	4	5
Rewards and sanctions are used effectively	1	2	3	4	5
Team members are clear about what is expected of them	1	2	3	4	5
Team decisions are implemented by all team members	1	2	3	4	5
Team meetings are used effectively	1	2	3	4	5
The team regularly evaluates its progress	1	2	3	4	5
Pupils and/or parents contribute to evaluation	1	2	3	4	5

4   How do you recognize a good team?

It is important to know where you stand and if you have arrived. A checklist against which you can test the state of development of your team is a useful evaluative tool. I am therefore including the 'Good-team checklist', developed for the Survival Guide series (Kemp and Nathan 1989). It is a general checklist, but is as relevant for a pastoral team as for a subject department.

CASE STUDY 4.1

For reflection

A good team checklist

4.1.1   *Shares clear objectives and agreed goals:*

- agrees on what the team is trying to do and its priorities for action;
- agrees on what differences are tolerable within the team;
- clarifies the role of team members;
- discusses values and reaches a general consensus on its underlying philosophy.

4.1.2   *Has clear procedures:*

- for holding meetings;
- for making decisions and delegating responsibility.

4.1.3 Reviews its progress regularly:

- reassesses its objectives;
- evaluates the processes that the team is using;
- does not spend too much time discussing the past.

4.1.4 Has leadership appropriate to its membership:

- the leader is visible and accessible;
- the leader utilizes the strengths of all the team members;
- the leader models the philosophy of the team.

4.1.5 Has open lines of communication

- team members talk to each other about issues, not just to the team leader;
- recognizes each person's contribution;
- gives positive and negative feedback;
- members are open-minded to other people's arguments;
- welcomes ideas and advice from outside the team;
- members are skilled in sending and receiving messages in face-to-face communication.

4.1.6 Has a climate of support and trust:

- members give and ask for support;
- members spend enough time together to function effectively;
- members' strengths are valued and built upon;
- there is respect for other people's views;
- relates positively to other teams and groups.

4.1.7 Recognizes that conflict is inevitable and can be constructive:

- issues are dealt with immediately and openly;
- members are assertive but not aggressive;
- feelings are recognized and dealt with;
- members are encouraged to contribute ideas;
- conflicting viewpoints are seen as normal and dealt with constructively.

4.1.8 Is concerned with its members' personal and career development:

- each team member receives a regular review;
- the leader looks for chances to develop the members and they to develop the leader.

Source: Kemp and Nathan (1989).

How do you evaluate how your year/house team is functioning as a team?

One way in which you can assess where you are now is to use the 'good-team checklist' as an evaluation document. Whereas the 'team audit' concentrates on how the team is performing, the 'good-team checklist' concentrates on the team itself. You may want to use it as an alternative to the team audit (p. 45), if so you could use it as an audit. In this case, first grade your team yourself on a 1–5 scale for each item. Then ask the members of the team to grade each item, then tabulate the results to see what picture emerges. It is more likely, however, that you will want to use it as the basis for a team discussion about its progress or consider specific items included in the checklist.

Select the time for this exercise carefully, it is very important that team members are prepared to be honest and are not paying off scores or past resentments. Similarly do not do it too soon as they may be too polite. If it is done properly, you should be able to see whether there is general agreement about the team. You can eliminate the obvious personal hang-ups because these will stand out from the other scores at one extreme or the other, but it is useful to know who feels like this. The results may reinforce what you had guessed, or may give you some surprises. It can be useful for both reasons, as long as you build on what it tells you.

An evaluation is a snapshot of where the team is now. It should be used as the first step towards improvement, so make sure that it is followed by an action plan, which builds on the information provided by the evaluation process, otherwise you could find that people will grudge the time that they have spent filling in the form. If it works for you, you will want to evaluate the team on a regular basis, perhaps annually.

5 What are the special features of managing a pastoral team?

In Chapter 1 some of the difficulties of managing a pastoral team were introduced. These included:

Lack of choice about who is put onto the team

- The extent to which you can influence the membership of your team and how much choice you get varies enormously from school to school. Often for all kinds of reasons, you get very little choice.
- The more effective you are as a year head, the more likely it is that you will be asked to take on weak or difficult colleagues as members of your team.

Case Study 4.2 is about handling a team with a number of problem members.

Reluctant and uncommitted team members

- Some team members are totally committed to their subject teaching and grudge the time that has to be spent on pastoral care and tutoring.
- Poor tutors – effective tutoring requires skill as well as effort.
- Overenthusiasm – some tutors rush into counselling with little understanding of what they are doing. These tutors can cause you endless extra work.

Lack of stability in the team

- Internal school politics may cause members to be moved into or out of your team after a year, which makes it difficult to team build.
- You may stay as head of, for example, Year 7, while your team may go up with their tutor groups, with the result that you are managing a different group of people every year.

Too little time for meetings/discussions with team members

- Managing time is a management issue for year heads and a major problem. It is dealt with in Chapter 3. Here it is worth noting that team meetings can be difficult to fit in. Not all the members may be able to attend and there are likely to be too many items on the agenda to be able to give each sufficient time to deal with them well. Informal lunch-hour sessions, which are a regular feature of departmental organization, can be more difficult for year heads to manage, partly because of your other commitments and partly because subject departments often sit together in the staffroom.

Your own lack of expertise

- For the team to run effectively, you have to inspire confidence as a leader, yet you are likely to have had little training in dealing with pastoral matters. As a year head, you have to prove yourself in the job and it will take time to gain the respect of your colleagues. Case Study 4.2 deals with this issue.

Because pastoral teams are so difficult to manage, you might want to think about some of the management issues. A list of questions to address is included below. Again you may wish to use this list to help you evaluate how your team is performing.

Team building – questions to address

- How much collaboration is there? Is collaborative action essential for achievement?
- As team leader are you familiar with and committed to team improvement?
- Is there a feeling that something needs to improve?
- Are the people willing to look at their own work and engage in problem-solving activities?
- What are the resource implications?
- Is there a willingness and capacity to give or receive feedback?
- Is there a sincere interest in change?
- Are minds made up as to the nature of problems and what must be done?
- Is there an openness to information and a willingness to move in the direction that any data suggests?

CASE STUDY 4.2

Taking over an existing team

Taking over an established team can be fraught with difficulties and can be particularly hard for an internal appointee. In this case study Joyotti Pattni has recently been appointed as a head of year. She is unhappy about the way that some members of her team are reacting to her appointment, especially the deputy head of year, James, who was also a candidate for the post and had expected to succeed. She discusses the problem with Eric Warne, Head of Year 10. She has been his deputy for the last 2 years; they get on well and he is acting as her mentor.

Although I am delighted to have got the job, especially as I didn't really expect to beat James Dixon, I am extremely concerned about how the team is reacting to my appointment. James is a particular worry. He is clearly very aggrieved about not getting the job and is not being at all co-operative. It seems to make him very negative about anything that I suggest. He can be extremely sarcastic and team meetings have been very difficult, because he rubbishes my suggestions. I suspect that he also resents my being a woman and Asian. The year team has worked together for quite a long time and is chauvinistic and rather set in its ways. My working methods are quite different from Mr Shelley's (he has just retired after 15 years in the post). My whole approach is far less formal and directive. I expect to consult the team about things and try to give everyone a chance to air his/her views. With this team, consulting seems to be treated as asking them to do my job for me. I'm not sure how to tackle the problem, or even how to define the problem precisely. I am due to hold another department meeting next week and am increasingly anxious about it . . .

For discussion

- What are the main issues here? Define the problem/s.
- What is Joyotti's preferred management style and how does it differ from her predecessor's? What problems does this create for her?
- If you were Joyotti Pattni how would you deal with James, a most unco-operative deputy head of year?
- What do you think are the main differences between being a deputy head of year/ second in department and being head of year/head of department?
- What stage of development has this team reached?
- What advice would you give Joyotti about reforming/developing the team?
- What management skills would you need to use effectively in order to resolve the problems?
- If you were Mrs Pattni how would you prepare for the next department meeting?

Mrs Pattni has a problem in gaining acceptance as teamleader. One team member clearly resents her appointment and is extremely unco-operative, largely because he himself wanted but failed to get the post, and also because he was a crony of the previous leader. James' view of things could influence how others think, and this could create difficulties for her. James fits into Bramson's (1981) stereotypes of difficult people as a hostile aggressive, whose persistent hostility and sarcasm could affect the performance of the team and erode Joyotti's own confidence. He cannot be allowed to continue to rubbish her suggestions and treat her disrespect-fully at department meetings. Sooner or later if she is to develop any kind of professional relationship with James, she must confront the situation. This will test her leadership and assertiveness skills. The session could easily become a row. However nasty James may be, Joyotti must not allow James' sarcasm to affect her, or let the discussion deteriorate into a slanging match. She must keep to issues, not personalities. She must think through what she wants to achieve from the session and manage it. It is a vital stage of the team-building process because if she succeeds, not only will James be able to work with her, but the team are likely to accept her leadership.

There are also some race and gender issues here. The disappointed candidate is reluctant to accept a woman as leader and especially an Asian woman. It is not clear how far this attitude is representative of the whole team. Even if this is not as big a problem as Mrs Pattni thinks it is, she thinks it is true, and this compounds the problem. The team is testing her out and she is certainly going to have to demonstrate her ability to command in order to gain the respect of this group. Indeed, the ability to take charge of the situation is central to success in handling difficult or unco-operative people. If assertiveness is an issue here, she should seek some training as she is going to have to show that she expects to succeed.

Her leadership style is very different from that of her predecessor. She describes it as collaborative, but the team seems to feel that she is abdicating her responsibility to direct it, which as far as the team is concerned means telling the team what to do. Even if her style is naturally collaborative, this may not be the most appropriate manage-ment style so early in the evolution of the group. They are used to a very directive style and are educated to think this is good leadership. In any case, early in the development of a team, you often have to be more directive than later on, so the advice to Joyotti is, for the time being, show that she can lead by having the ideas and using the 'tell' approach. As she establishes herself, the two sides begin to know each other better and mutual confidence grows, there will be plenty of opportunity for consultation.

The team is established, but it appears set in its ways and resistant to change. It is also finding the change of leadership traumatic. Joyotti will have to decide whether she wants to be a gradualist or a Draconian. There is not a clear-cut answer here, as it could be argued that she would be well advised to wait until the team is more amenable before she makes major changes, because they could easily wreck any initiatives that she tries to introduce, and then blame her for the failure. Yet there is a case for asserting herself as a leader. Indeed, if there are changes that it is important to make now, she should do so. The team will be expecting some change, even if it is determined to resist on principle. What is important is to choose her battleground with care and prepare well. If she can establish herself as the manager of successful change, she will earn respect and, next time, it will be much easier to introduce changes.

Quite frequently there is an internal unsuccessful and resentful candidate, so when you take over a year group, you could find yourself in a similar situation to Joyotti. If so, remember that there are techniques that you can use that will help you in dealing with a difficult member of staff. It would be sensible to look for a colleague, either at your own level or among the senior staff who will mentor and support you while you deal with the problem. It always helps if there is someone who will listen to you – sharing a problem helps reduce its size. It is even better if, because of his/her knowledge of the school and/or the individual concerned, s/he can give you some sensible advice. In Joyotti's case she is using her ex-year head, with whom she had a good relationship, as a mentor and a sounding board.

If none of these strategies work, then she may want to think about moving someone, probably James, out of the team at the end of the year. Although you get less choice about the choice of team members than if you are a subject leader, it is actually easier to change the make-up of a pastoral team than that of a subject department. You cannot move a French teacher to the mathematics department, but you can move a tutor into another year group. Cutting the knot could be the solution for both James and Joyotti. Without James the team is likely to be more amenable and a new team member will change the dynamics of the situation.

6 What roles do people play in teams?

Belbin (1981) claims that one of the key determinants to a team's success is the nature of the interaction in terms of the qualities brought to carrying out a task. He argues that status, technical knowledge and experience are not necessarily the most significant determinants of an individual's contribution. In fact what he calls the 'alpha team' (i.e. a team which is entirely composed of high achievers) may perform significantly less well than one made up according to his criteria for effective task management. Belbin identifies eight role types, which refer to the potential contribution of the individual in terms of behaviour or roles rather than knowledge or status. They are:

- *chair/co-ordinator* – controls and directs the team, is able to make best use of its diverse talents and balance contributions in order to secure the goals and objectives (*characteristics:* stable and dominant);
- *shaper* – pushes the team onwards towards an action, sets objectives and looks for outcomes (*characteristics:* dominant, extrovert and anxious);
- *plant* – innovates, generates new ideas and approaches, problem solver (*characteristics:* intelligent and introvert);
- *resource investigator* – the team's contact with its environment, generates ideas and resources (*characteristics:* intelligent, stable and introvert);
- *monitor/evaluator* – analyses problems and evaluates contributions (*characteristics:* stable and introvert);
- *completer/finisher* – ensures attention to detail, maintains schedules (*characteristics:* anxious and introvert);
- *company worker/implementer* – capable of converting plans into action working systematically and efficiently (*characteristics:* stable and controlled);
- *teamworker* – supports and reinforces, improves communications, fosters team spirit (*characteristics:* stable, extrovert and flexible).

Belbin's analysis is frequently used on management courses and may be known to you. Briefly, each member of the team fills in an individual questionnaire, which is then analysed to identify the dominant roles adopted by each member of the team and used to help identify the strengths in roles within the team. If the team is confident enough, there is a further stage of analysis. In this second stage, members of the team fill in Belbin questionnaires on each other, and these are then analysed. This helps the team understand their perceptions of each other.

Role analysis is a useful management tool because it highlights whether a team has a good balance of roles or whether there is imbalance or overlap (e.g. a frequent problem is that there are too many teamworkers, but no plant or ideas person).

How can a pastoral leader use the Belbin analysis?

Initially there would appear to be a problem for you because, as a pastoral leader with less control over team selection than a subject leader, you will not be able to use the analysis as much as a department head may do when making appointments. It would not be surprising if you find this frustrating. Nevertheless, having this knowledge can actually help the team function more effectively. Being aware of the gaps makes you think about strategies to overcome the problem.

One strategy is to help individuals develop their second- and third-string characteristics. People very rarely have only one dominant characteristic. Often the results are quite close and you could use this to help fill gaps in the team.

If you fill in the questionnaire more than once because you are the member of a number of different teams, you may well find that you get different results. This is because people play different roles in different teams. In one team you may be the co-ordinator, in another a shaper, in a third a teamworker. This is because of the different composition and needs of the three teams. As a pastoral leader, you must be able to build on the fact that people do play different roles in different teams

CASE STUDY 4.3

For action/discussion

Welding individuals into a team

You are an experienced team leader, but you have been asked to take over a large and more complex pastoral team, which includes some difficult people and does not work well together. The team includes:

- someone who wanted the job and is aggrieved at your promotion;
- a head of faculty who considers himself much too busy to bother with pastoral issues. He could be helpful, but isn't. Indeed, he can be very difficult and disobliging at times. He dodges your meetings and generally does as little as possible;
- a team member who knows it all with a tendency to do his own thing regardless of what you say;

- two members of the team who really don't get on. Team meetings can be very acrimonious;
- a persistent worrier who refers everything to you;
- a burned-out teacher, who has a growing pattern of absence, and who is beginning to attract parental complaints. His tutor group is becoming noisy and attracting adverse comments from other staff;
- a team member who regards team meetings as an opportunity to say what he thinks and comes with his own agenda. His contributions, which you rarely find helpful, take up a lot of meeting time;
- a newly qualified teacher, with lots of ideas to offer, who is impatient with and inclined to skip some essential department procedures, and whose relationship with her form is becoming too cosy.

For discussion

This may be an extreme example of a difficult team, but, even if you don't have to deal with a whole team like this, some of the individuals could easily turn up in your team.

- What are the issues here facing you as team leader?
- What techniques and management style would it be most effective for you to employ?
- How can you weld this group of people together?
- You want to introduce some major changes – how can you ensure that you manage this effectively?

Welding

Some very difficult people are members of this team and it is not working well together, so how do you deal with it? Adopt a positive attitude – you expect to win this situation, although it may take time and you will have to persevere. Your own attitude to the problem will affect your likelihood of success. Some strategies to consider:

- divide and rule – if it is too difficult to deal with everyone at once, decide whom to target first and talk individually to each member of the team;
- make use of individuals' strengths, or their weaknesses, dependent on the needs of the team;
- don't have too many meetings if they are too difficult. Make sure, however, that you do continue to communicate. When you do have meetings use the structures and agenda to help you;
- you need some allies on the team – they don't all dislike you, even if they dislike each other. In the case of the two enemies, talking individually to each about working for the good of the team might help. They may not want to let you down;
- if a head of faculty/senior member of staff is part of your team start with a softly-softly approach and ask for his support as a senior member of staff. This is important as you

may need to show that you have done the 'right' thing, but sooner or later you will have to confront the situation and insist that his/her professional duties are carried out and that your meetings are attended. Before you take this approach, talk the issue through with your line manager and make sure that you will be supported as the Head of Faculty will be on a higher scale than you – without support, you could be humiliated;

- another line you could take is to put the item/s, for which the unproductive team member had responsibility, on the agenda at each meeting and each time ask for a verbal report on progress. It could shame the person sufficiently to make him/her do at least part of the job;

- target the NQT – important as a younger teacher is more improvable than an older one and you need some loyalty and you don't want the NQT to gang up with some of the unimprovably difficult characters;

- if a member of the team persistently comes to meetings with his/her own agenda and takes over, use your position power as chairperson to keep the meeting on schedule. If the problem persists, keep notes on the number of interruptions and their effect on the team and at a private meeting with the team member spell out that there were, for example, ten interruptions in an hour's meeting and that only two were constructive. What does s/he propose to do to remedy the matter as the situation is damaging the team and making him/her unpopular. Suggest INSET (in service education and training) if necessary! If all else fails, put it in writing with a copy to some powerful people (e.g. your line manager);

- helping a worrier – make sure that all communications are very clear and that the worrier understands at all times what is expected of him/her (i.e. ensure that there are as few uncertainties as possible). Nevertheless, this person will take up time and you need to think through strategies that will lessen his/her anxieties while not taking up all your free time. Via the person's appraiser, try to make a target and perhaps set up some INSET for confidence building;

- use team-building activities. A team-building exercise, using specific INSET time for team building (e.g. a day/weekend off the premises, possibly with an outside facilitator), could be beneficial for the team. As there are cost implications, do think carefully about what the team would gain most from this;

- joint planning, working together as a team on a planning session, is in itself a team-building exercise. Think carefully about how you can do this, so that you avoid the problems created by some of the team members;

- when things begin to improve a bit, build regular sessions to discuss the state of the team into the programme of meetings. Creating an atmosphere in which people can say what they really feel will build up trust and strengthen the team. This should not be an excuse for unnecessary criticisms of others. Monitor the sessions carefully and do not allow them to go on too long – a guillotine could be useful!

CASE STUDY 4.4

For action/discussion

I used to have such a good team ...

Up till a year ago I really enjoyed being a team leader. I had built up and developed my team until it had reached the 'performing stage'. All the team members were extremely capable, there was a high level of trust and we worked most effectively together as a team. If I delegated a task, it would be seen as a development opportunity for a member of the team, there was always a positive reaction and the team members prided themselves in making a good job of it. When two of them said that they wanted to widen their experience by working in the lower team before going for deputy-headship, of course I encouraged them, but I didn't anticipate the impact that two new members would have on my team. I expected to be able to train them in the same way that I had done with the original team members, and that they would quickly be absorbed into the team, but it didn't work out like that at all. The old and new team members didn't empathize at all and the team after 10 months still doesn't jell; indeed, I seem to be back in the storming stage of team building. It has been like this for months and I am not enjoying it at all. One of the new people is particularly unco-operative a real know-all, without the expertise to manage to do what he claims he can do, and the other is an enthusiast who diverts the team from tried and tested routes, and railroads us into taking on board schemes which sound OK, but which in practice rarely work, and then cause us more problems. I'm at my wit's end over the situation ...

(An upper team leader at a primary school bewails the effect on her team of some changes in staff)

For discussion

- What are the main issues involved in this case study?
- What state of formation is this team in?
- What advice would you give this team leader?

For action

Apply the problem-solving model to this case study.

BIBLIOGRAPHY AND FURTHER READING

Belbin, M. (1981) *Management Teams: Why They Succeed or Fail*, London: Heinemann.

Bramson, R. H. (1981) *Coping with Difficult People*, New York: Bantam, Doubleday.

Kemp, R. and Nathan, M. (1989) *Middle Management in Schools, A Survival Guide*, Oxford: Blackwell.

Katzenbach, J. and Smith, D. (1993) *The Wisdom of Teams*, New York: Harper Business.

Trethowan, D. (1985) *Teamwork, Industrial Society, Management in Schools and Colleges*, Pamphlet series, London: Industrial Society.

Chapter 5

Managing and developing your tutor team

In the previous chapter I discussed the team as a whole, now I want to consider how to get the best from the individual tutors in your team. This constitutes one of the main challenges for you as a year head or pastoral leader. The main reason why it is so difficult is that while you may have one or two really good tutors on your team, several may leave much to be desired, either because they lack motivation and commitment, or they do not have the ability to do the job well.

LACK OF MOTIVATION

Few tutors are enthused about being tutors. Many simply consider it as yet more work. Managing reluctant tutors is an ongoing problem for year or house heads. Usually the reluctant tutors constitute the minority of the team, but they take up a disproportionate amount of your time, and challenge your authority as a leader. Case Study 5.8 discusses this problem.

LACK OF EXPERTISE AMONG THE TEAM MEMBERS

Naturally good tutors do exist, but in small numbers. Tutoring is a skill which needs developing; however, there is little training available for tutors, and, even if there were more, the tutors, who most need it, would be least likely to apply for it. Tight INSET (in-service education and training) budgets don't help, because, with the development of the category of expert teacher, colleagues are much more likely to choose a training session which will help them consolidate their subject skills, than a session to help them enhance their tutoring skills. This means that developing the tutoring skills of your team is down to you and this is no easy task. For this reason, this chapter aims to present you with some materials that you could use or adapt when working with your tutors, and with some detailed case studies, so that you can compare these scenarios and possible solutions with your own team's problems.

The first step is to define what you mean by good tutoring. It is easy enough to identify poor tutoring, but how do you recognize good tutoring? Case Study 5.1 provides an exemplar of good practice. It describes a good tutor and the effect he had on his tutor group over a relatively short period of time.

CASE STUDY 5.1

Recognizing effective tutoring – an exemplar of good practice

When Phil was asked to take on the tutor group, it had a bad reputation. Over the last year, under a weak tutor, who has now left the school, the behaviour of the class had deteriorated. In class the pupils were inattentive with a poor concentration span. They interrupted each other in order to say what they thought, and rarely listened to what others had to say, regardless of whether it was the teacher or other pupils. Relationships within the group were poor. The headteacher was particularly concerned over Donovan, one of the small number of Afro-Caribbean pupils, because, although, when teachers looked out from the staffroom window onto the playground, it appeared that Donovan was mixing well with a group of white boys, in fact it transpired that he was experiencing a form of bullying, which was essentially racist. It had become bad enough for Donovan to start to truant, and he had been brought back into school by his father, who wanted to know what the school was doing to stop incidents of this sort. There had also recently been a nasty altercation between two of the girls, which had brought complaints from both sets of parents. Something clearly needed to be done about the tutor group, and Phil, who was known to have an excellent rapport with the pupils of all ages, was asked to take on the group and to apply positive tutoring strategies.

Towards the end of the year, when the school was inspected, the class who consistently drew positive comments from the inspection team was Phil's tutor group. The group was unrecognizable to anyone who had known their earlier history. In Phil's own English lesson, the inspectors commented on how well the pupils listened to each other and the quality of the discussion. A very able Chinese boy had written the best poem. The group listened attentively, while he read his work aloud, then spontaneously they applauded. The discussion which followed indicated how well they had listened, because they could identify all the good points in the poem and make appropriate critical judgements. Only a few months ago, not only would they not have listened, but there was a good chance that Yan's book would have gone missing or been mutilated. In afternoon registration, the pupils answered to their name in Chinese, and the inspectors were told that this happened once a week, and that a regular opportunity had been built into the Personal, Social and Health Education (PSHE) programme for pupils to learn some Chinese, with Yan as their teacher.

In discussion with the inspector, who visited the tutor period, pupils consistently mentioned the unobtrusive support given to them by their tutor, especially in helping them reconcile their differences and, indeed, the quality of relationships within the group and with the tutor were particularly noticed by the inspection team. The lay inspector, who was looking into pupil behaviour and welfare, reported back that a group of year-9 pupils had set up an interesting self-help scheme for years 7–9 to help pupils cope with bullying and other difficulties. The lead turned out to be being taken by Phil's tutor group with Yan, Donovan and Susan as the main organizers.

During the lunch hour the inspectors found a group of pupils taking responsibility for looking after the guinea pigs and cleaning the pond. They too proved to be members of Phil's tutor group, and amongst the leaders were Katie and Susan, the two girls who had been involved in the altercation last year. Now they were working amicably together. The form's contribution to a recent charity event had been to run a open-air cafe on the patio in the area near the staffroom. This had proved so popular that there had been a request that it should open on a regular basis for charity. Similarly, a very popular after-school martial-arts activity not only involved most of the group, but had expanded to include pupils from other year groups and now also attracted adult recruits from the village, who had heard about it from their children. It was now becoming so big that a second session was being organized, with another teacher helping Phil.

For discussion

- What were the main differences in the behaviour of the group over time?
- What kind of strategies had Phil adopted with his tutor group and with what success?
- What are the issues involved in this case study?
- What are the lessons of this case study for you as a tutor-team manager?
- Think about your own tutor team. Who stand out as good tutors? What is it that they are they doing that makes them good tutors?
- What is the effect of one good tutor on the rest of your team?
- Using this case study as a prompt can you construct a list of positive tutoring strategies?

The case study provides us with an example of good tutoring, so what are the positive features to be found here?

- The tutor's clear commitment to his task.
- The thought given to finding suitable challenging activities, which would help his tutor group develop their social skills.
- The provision of a variety of ways in which pupils could take responsibility.
- The clear standard of what is acceptable behaviour.
- The unobtrusive, but persistent support for individuals to help them reconcile their differences and work constructively together.
- Sensitive development of the pupils' listening skills.
- The emphasis on creating a good atmosphere in the form and a positive group entity.

CASE STUDY 5.2

For reflection

Sometimes the bonding is too personal

We had a problem when an inspirational tutor died. Tom was a brilliant tutor, so much so that we had developed a habit of putting a lot of hard cases into his tutor group. Not only could he control them, when others could not, but, by the end of the year, the progress made by these pupils, in terms of their willingness to learn and ability to work with others, was always very noticeable and when he took a tutor group up for 5 years, the effects were significant. Last year, in January, only a week or so after the Christmas holiday, Tom had a massive heart attack, and he died. We were all shocked and distressed, of course, but his year-9 tutor group became a major problem for us, because it refused to accept a substitute tutor and created hell for the poor teacher, who came in as supply until we could get a permanent replacement for Tom. In the end, the headteacher had to take the group over personally until the end of the summer term and we restructured the tutor groups for the following year. They were going into year 10 and we used this as an excuse . . .

It could be helpful in understanding what good tutoring means by comparing Phil, who is clearly a very effective tutor, with a tutor who is involved but less good at carrying out the role.

CASE STUDY 5.3

Meryl, an NQT, joined your tutor team at the beginning of the Autumn term. As she was a last-minute appointment, there was no opportunity to give consideration to where she would fit best, she simply had to fill the gap. She seemed to have established a good initial rapport with the year-10 group, but, as time passed, you become increasingly worried about her over-close relationship with some of the pupils and the general standard of behaviour of the form. Colleagues comment that the pupils arrive to lessons late from tutor time and appear overexcited, and that their formroom is left in a mess. You have a word with her about this, and for a time things improve, but soon the adverse staff comments begin again. This time when you speak to Meryl, she is defensive, claiming that she is fulfilling her duties as a tutor well. She is very critical of the short time available for tutor time. The discussion becomes almost acrimonious, as she does not appear to want to understand how the situation is viewed by others, and begins to take the attitude that the school (by which she means you) cares more about some petty rules than about people.

During this discussion, she mentions a problem within the group with which she is dealing. She offers this information as one of the reasons why more tutor time is needed. You are concerned that she appears to be tackling a quite serious problem without consultation and worried about the quality of 'advice' she appears to be offering one of the girl pupils, Mary. Trying to be tactful, and aware that the fault probably lies in her inexperience, you do not tell her to stop dealing with the problem. You insist however, that you must monitor the situation, that she must report regularly, accept advice from you or the deputy for pastoral matters, and that normal procedures must be followed. She appears to accept this ruling, but it soon becomes clear that she is telling you as little as possible and continuing to act unilaterally. Colleagues mention seeing Meryl on a number of occasions recently in the lunch hour in the playground, in a quiet place behind the gymnasium, talking at length to the pupil, Mary. They are curious about what is going on, and disapproving. When you remonstrate with Meryl, she talks about the need to respect the girl's confidence and admits that she has promised Mary not to tell anyone.

For discussion

Meryl is convinced that she is a good tutor. Her year head and other staff disagree. She is clearly putting a lot of effort into her tutoring, but she is not regarded by her colleagues as an effective tutor.

- What major mistakes has Meryl made?
- What advice would you give the tutor?
- How would you get her to accept your good advice?
- What advice would you give this year head?
- With whom should the year head liaise when dealing with this situation.
- What action should the year head take immediately. What should the long-term strategy be?
- The relationship between the year head and the tutor appears to be breaking down. How can the year head retrieve this situation?

TUTORS SHOULD KNOW WHAT THE EXPECTATIONS ARE

It is axiomatic that you cannot expect your tutors to do the job simply by instinct. They need to know what is expected of them. They should have a clear job description. Case Study 5.4 is a typical example of a form tutor's job description.

CASE STUDY 5.4

Exemplar for comparision

Bestwick Park High School – form tutor's job description

Most members of staff are asked to act as form tutors. The role of the form tutor is a responsible one and vital to the efficient running of the school and to successful pastoral care.

For this aspect of the work, the form tutor is responsible to the head of year. The main functions are as follows:

5.4.1 Registration and routine business

The form tutor is responsible for the accurate daily marking of the form register (a vital legal document) and for seeing that all the information in the register is maintained up to date. Other returns of a routine nature should be dealt with as required, together with the distribution of information to parents. All absences must be accounted for by notes and any not so covered should be reported to the year head.

5.4.2 Reports and records

The form tutor is responsible for the duplicate copies of reports. Any information of a confidential nature should be referred to the year head. The form tutor is expected to comment on reports and cover aspects of achievement and personality, which are not covered by academic reports.

5.4.3 References and special reports

When appropriate, form tutors are expected to prepare, in consultation with colleagues, initial drafts for references, testimonials and special reports to outside agencies and the like.

5.4.4 Personal appearance and conduct

Form tutors are expected to monitor the personal appearance, e.g. wearing of correct uniform, and behaviour of the members of their form and to insist on a reasonable standard.

5.4.5 Homework

In consultation with the head of year, form tutors should draw up a homework timetable for their form, and, from time to time, check that it is adhered to satisfactorily by all pupils.

5.4.6 Form time

This time should be used purposefully and profitably in accordance with the programme of activities drawn up by the head of year and the member of staff with special responsibility for the PSHE programme. THE FORM SHOULD REMAIN WITH THE FORM TUTOR IN THE ROOM ASSIGNED TO IT THROUGHOUT THIS PERIOD.

5.4.7 Assemblies

FORM TUTORS ARE EXPECTED TO ATTEND ASSEMBLIES WITH THEIR FORM AND TO SUPERVISE THE FORM'S MOVEMENT TO AND FROM THE FORMROOM TO THE PLACE OF THE ASSEMBLY.

5.4.8 Year meetings

Form tutors are expected to attend meetings as arranged in the school calendar and any others which might be necessary, as called by the head of year.

5.4.9 Relations with parents

It is hoped that parents would see form tutors at parents' meetings. Whenever possible form tutors will be involved when parents visit the school at other times. Form tutors should not arrange to see parents without reference to the head of year, who will consult senior staff before making any arrangements.

The form tutor should be the first person to whom a pupil will turn for help or advice, although it may be necessary to refer the matter to the year head, deputy head pastoral, head teacher or matron. Although some aspects of a form tutor's work may seem dull and routine, it is through regular daily contact that unobtrusive care is exercised.

Notes (same as Subject Teacher's job description. They reserve the SMT's right to change items).

The Bestwick Park form tutor's job description is a typical example of how a school views the role. It does not make easy reading, yet it does make it clear what the school expects of its tutors. The nine tasks set out in the job description describe:

- when you are expected to be with your form (e.g. at registration, in form time and at assembly). Being with the form during assembly and form time is highlighted by the use of capital letters. The school is stressing the importance of this task and hinting that there have been problems in the past;
- what a tutor's responsibilities are (e.g. keeping registers accurately, seeing to the reports, distributing and collecting information, sorting out the form's homework timetable and monitoring uniform);
- what meetings tutors are expected to attend (e.g. year meetings and parents' evenings).

There are, however, some things that it does not clearly define (e.g. it does not say what to do in form time, except that it needs to be used purposefully and profitably and that tutors have to make sure that the pupils do not leave the formroom and wander about the school).

Sometimes it is deliberately vague. For example, it mentions that the tutor should follow the programme of activities drawn up by the year head or PSHE co-ordinator, which implies that a tutor will be teaching the form's PSHE. It carefully avoids saying, however, that this means that the tutor will be teaching the PSHE or what it will involve, yet this is a sensitive area about which your tutors will need a lot of information. Similarly, it emphasizes that it is not prescribing how much time the various tasks will take and that it may not have listed everything, yet you will notice that it insists that form tutor's duties are included in directed time, thus making them a compulsory part of the job. Thus there is a strong hint in the job description that there is more to being a form tutor than carrying out the tasks enumerated on this list.

What this job description does not show you very clearly is that in fact the form tutor's role covers three main areas of responsibility:

- *responsibility for the routine administration of the form;*
- *responsibility for the good conduct of the form;*
- *responsibility for the pastoral care of the form.*

In addition the form tutor may have to teach PSHE to his/her form. The functions, listed at length in the Bestwick Park job description, summarize most of the tasks connected with the first two aspects of the role and put most emphasis on the routine administration. Pastoral care is barely mentioned; it is implicit rather than explicit. Indeed, the only mention is of 'unobtrusive care' and, whereas this may reflect this particular school's priorities, it also indicates how the job actually works. A lot of a tutor's time will be spent on routine business, because this does ensure the smooth and efficient running of the school, yet every now and then a pastoral issue will emerge which will need sensitive handling.

For reflection or discussion

Comment on the job description. How does it compare with the tutor's job description used in your school? Is it a good idea to keep pastoral care implicit rather than explicit? You can argue this one both ways!

To get the best from your tutor team, you may need to draw up your own job description. Make it succinct rather than wordy, so that the important ideas are clearly stated. The headings mentioned in Case Study 5.4 could provide the basis for the job description (Figure 5.1). You could put bullet points relevant to your school below each heading.

Writing the job description yourself makes it yours, not theirs – yet another top-down exercise. Writing it together with your team makes it 'ours' and gives the team some ownership. This is why it is a good idea to start with headings. You have clearly set the agenda, but have not written it for them. Producing a tutor's job description together could be a very useful team-building exercise for you and your tutors as well as enhancing understanding of the role.

What is important is how you prepare the ground for this exercise. First, you must be clear what you want to achieve, otherwise the whole exercise is pointless. This does not mean that you should railroad your ideas through, rather that you need to have a clear idea of what really matters and on what issues you are prepared to make concessions.

Case Study 5.5 is designed to help you focus your team on the issue of what makes good tutoring. If you use this before you try to write the job description, it could making the writing task much easier, as its purpose is to seek agreement on the fundamentals of the job. The list is not sacrosanct. Change or rewrite items to fit your needs.

Job description: form tutor

The form tutor's role covers three main areas of responsibility:

1   responsibility for the routine administration of the form

-
-

2   responsibility for the good conduct of the form

-
-

3   responsibility for the pastoral care of the form

-
-

It might also be helpful to write short sections on:
- managing form time;
- delivering the PSHE curriculum.

Figure 5.1 Your own job description.

CASE STUDY 5.5

For discussion with your tutor team

Tutors must ...

1. Tutors must provide a safe environment for the pupils in their form.
2. Tutors must care.
3. Tutors must enforce the uniform code consistently.
4. Tutors must be included.
5. Tutors must tell pupils that they cannot promise confidentiality.
6. Tutors must be impartial.
7. Tutors must be responsible for the good behaviour of their tutor group.
8. Tutors must be consulted.
9. Tutors must ensure that routine procedures are carried out.
10. Tutors must keep to deadlines.
11. Tutors must be the linchpin.
12. Tutors must be set realistic targets.
13. Tutors must monitor homework diaries regularly.
14. Tutors must be allowed opinions.
15. Tutors must adhere to school procedures.
16. Tutors must distribute documents and collect in returns promptly.

17. Tutors must do their job.
18. Tutors must protect children.
19. Tutors must encourage the pupils to take a pride in the appearance of their uniform and the classroom.
20. Tutors must liaise with section heads or senior management if major concerns arise.
21. Tutors must contribute to the PSHE programme.
22. Tutors must allow pupils to undertake appropriate responsibilities.
23. Tutors must ensure that pupils keep a good balance between academic work, extra-curricular and other activities.
24. Tutors must accept that sometimes a pupil will choose to turn to others in preference to them.

Implementation problems

A crucial management issue, if you have put in the work to draft your own tutor's job description, is how to implement it if your school already has an unsatisfactory one. If your job description is informal, you could face problems with just those tutors who most need the job description. They will claim that it is not the real job description so that they do not have to follow it.

Get the support of the senior management team (SMT)

The understanding and clear support of your own pastoral line manager is particularly important, because, if you are supported by the SMT, it becomes more difficult for individual tutors to object. If your new tutors' job description is good enough, you may be able to get the school to adopt it.

The year heads should speak with one voice

It could also be useful if the year-head team spend some time together working to define the tutor's role. Not only will you all speak with one voice, but working together will help you generate ideas that you want to include in the job description. Good interpersonal skills are essential for a pastoral leader, who spends much of his/her time dealing with defensive or unmotivated people. In this instance tact and determination are the important qualities. Remember that skills can be developed over time and that if your interpersonal skills are a weakness, you should work to improve them.

HOW DO WE KNOW WHERE WE ARE?

Case Study 5.6 is another item which you could use with your tutor team. This item considers the role of the form tutor and asks the individual to evaluate how s/he thinks the role is perceived in the school. Its use is to make the tutor think about tutoring in the school. It can also be used as a group activity, because, if the team members agree, you can tabulate the team's results and use them as the basis of some forward planning. You may also want to discuss the results with the SMT as there will be implications for it.

CASE STUDY 5.6

For action

Role of the form tutor

Where are you now?

Evaluate your perception of your role as a form tutor by ringing one of the statements in each of the rows A–K.

Ascendant	Neutral	Subordinate
A Tutor obliged to have access to all information on pupils	Information mostly available on request	Tutor not given confidential information on pupils
B Tutor vital part of admission and induction process	Tutor fully informed in advance that new pupils will arrive	New pupils sent to join group without prior notification
C Subject teachers contact tutor in the first instance	Subject teachers sometimes keep tutors in touch, but not always	Subject teachers always go straight to pastoral head in serious cases
D Letters written home by tutor on his/her own initiative	Tutor can suggest letter is required	Tutor not normally shown pastoral head's correspondence
E Tutor basically responsible for attendance, calling for help when the need is felt	Pastoral head follows up absence queries initiated by tutor	Tutor merely marks the absences in the register and takes no further action
F Tutor plays major advisory role in vocational decisions	Tutor's assessment noted in writing	All vocational and educational advice centralized
G Tutor present at all major interviews with parents, careers staff, advisory personnel, welfare officers, etc.	Tutor told what took place at the interview	Tutor not informed such interviews are to happen

H Tutor's views usually solicited by senior staff before a pupil is seen by them	Tutor informed reasonably fully of any action by senior staff	Summary action taken by senior staff without notification to tutor
I Tutor keeps responsibility for the group throughout their school career	Tutors may follow the group if they express a strong wish to do so	Tutors assigned to groups on an 'ad hoc' basis or for administrative convenience
J Tutor designs his/her own 'pastoral curriculum' within the overall scheme	Tutors have input into the scheme, but do not design it	Tutors given all the worksheets, etc. and expected to 'do it', or the school has no pastoral curriculum
K Tutor feels the primary responsibility for his/her group	Tutor feels s/he has a significant input into the pastoral care system	Tutor feels that s/he is basically a register checker

When you have completed the chart, compare your results with the person next to you.

Source: Pearce (adapted from Marland).

CASE STUDY 5.7

It's the third time that I've caught David Rose skiving off assembly. I've put him in detention for Monday evening, but it's really Leslie, his tutor, that I'd like to put into detention. If he accompanied his form to assembly, David wouldn't be able to dodge off like that. When I mentioned to Leslie that I'd caught David, he looked surprised and said that they were all there, as far as he knew, when they left the formroom, but he had needed to collect something from the staffroom, so he hadn't gone downstairs with them. I was cross enough to point out that it wasn't the first time it had happened and eventually he said that he would keep an eye on David. I suspect that even if he set out with the whole class, Leslie would not know how many he still had on arrival, and that others beside David are skipping off on the way. David is simply not very good at getting away with it. Although he may be new to your tutor team, Leslie has been here for 3 years now, yet he still seems to be wet behind the ears.

A duty team leader, grumbles to the year head about a member of his tutor team.

For discussion

- What are the issues involved in this case study?
- What should be done about (1) David, (2) the problem of pupils skipping assembly?
- What advice would you give the year head in dealing with Leslie?

In the short term

Dealing with the pupils is a short-term problem

As the line manager you will need to monitor closely whether members of the tutor group are skipping assembly. It is almost a matter of counting them in and counting them out. The pupils, who tend to be quite bright about these things, will quickly cotton on that you are aware that sometimes some of them don't complete the journey to assembly. At least in the short term, they are likely to amend their behaviour, especially if you or a colleague regularly check the toilets and other known hiding places and pop into their formroom a little while after the others have left, just to see if anyone is there. Imposing a detention or some other appropriate punishment for skipping assembly will also send messages to the pupils. If they know that they will not be able to get away with skiving off assembly, are likely to get caught and that they will be punished, the game becomes less attractive.

In the long term

Dealing with the tutor is a far more difficult issue. This tutor is not performing to an acceptable standard. If this kind of problem occurs, you will have more information than is given here in a short case study. What follows is a guide to how to deal with problems of this sort rather than a specific answer to this problem.

Defining and analysing the problem

When dealing with the issue of performance, one of the first questions that you have to ask yourself is: What is this problem about? Defining and analysing the problem correctly is important, otherwise your solutions will be inappropriate. In this case the problem centres round what happens when the form goes to assembly. One pupil has been caught skipping assembly and it looks as if others are also truanting from assembly. What you don't know at this stage is what else they may have been doing.

Collecting the data

The more information you have, the better you will be able to deal with the problem, and your observation of how the tutor group is behaving will tell you a lot about how the tutor is performing. You will need, however, to monitor the tutor group's behaviour generally so that you can tell whether the problem is specific to assembly or the tip of an iceberg.

You want to know how regularly Leslie fails to accompany his form. If David Rose has been caught skiving off assembly three times, there will be other times when he was not caught, so does it mean that Leslie is extremely unobservant, or that he does other jobs at this time.

If you haven't popped into his tutor group during registration or form time recently, you would certainly want to do so in the near future, as you will have to establish what happens then. Questions to which you need answers include: What is Leslie's standard of discipline like and what kind of relationship does he have with his tutor group? You will also have to think about what effect your dealing with the pupils, rather than the tutor, is having on his relationship with them.

Establishing the cause

Then you have to ask yourself: Why is this problem occurring? Is Leslie a generally weak tutor or is this a specific problem?

The duty team leader has caught David three times. This means that he sees this as an ongoing, not a new problem, so it is unlikely that something has occurred to turn a good tutor into a less good one. This means that the cause is unlikely to be external.

You have to distinguish between 'can't and won't'. It is not quite clear in this case whether Leslie is simply a very weak tutor in terms of controlling his tutor group or whether, for some reason, which may be connected to his attitude to assembly, he does not want to do this part of his job. Is he simply oblivious, or doesn't he care?

The duty team leader describes Leslie as 'wet behind the ears' which suggests that s/he thinks this is a case of 'can't'. Indeed, the implication is that although he has been in the school for 3 years, Leslie is still making the classic mistakes of a new teacher. On the other hand, the tutor does not seem very bothered by the criticism, which has implications about his whole attitude to his job.

It could be the case that the problem is linked to his performance as a subject teacher. Perhaps Leslie's lessons are not as well prepared as his head of department requires, or he is not managing his time well and he is nipping off on the way to assembly to do some subject preparation. You will have to monitor whether he actually arrives at assembly, or whether he is using this time for other things. You may need to liaise with Leslie's subject manager and get an overall view of his performance.

There are other implications for you as Leslie's line manager. Leslie is a new member of your team, and you do not appear to have developed any professional relationship with him. If it is early in the academic year, you may not have realized that he is not carrying out all his responsibilities as conscientiously or as effectively as you would like. Nevertheless, you have a management responsibility both for the good conduct of the form and for Leslie in his capacity as the tutor. In a real situation there should be no surprises. Your day-to-day monitoring of your year group should have indicated clearly what kind of tutor Leslie is turning out to be. If things are not going as well as they should be, you have to take remedial action. All too frequently, either because you don't want a reputation as a tyrant or because there are major problems which are very time consuming, the minor failings are tolerated. The advice here is that you have a much better chance of rectifying the situation if you deal with it promptly. Untreated minor problems have a tendency to develop into major problems.

The interview with Leslie

You must certainly let Leslie know that you have been informed about the incident. Whereas this information may worry Leslie, it is better than suddenly requesting an interview about an incident that he does not realize you know about.

Sooner or later, preferably after you have collected sufficient data to know what you are dealing with, you will have to have a 'heart to heart' with Leslie. How you handle this is vital to your chances of improving his performance as a tutor. Although this is often difficult in a school because of the lack of small rooms which are not visible to all, make sure that you have privacy and that you have allowed sufficient time to explore the issues in depth. Rushing things or having to stop just when Leslie is beginning to open up could be counter-productive.

When the duty team leader told Leslie about David Rose, Leslie made an excuse. This is a typical response. You know, however, that this incident is not the first of its kind and you want to hear Leslie's explanation of why he is not accompanying his class to assembly. You must expect him to be defensive and there is a good chance that he will not tell you the truth. You will need all your skill at drawing him out.

The aim of the interview is to establish that you both recognize a problem and agree what the problem is. Your chances of modifying and improving Leslie's performance are better if you work collaboratively rather than simply give him orders.

Whether in this first session you are able to start to generate solutions depends on the difficulty of the problem and the time available. At this stage it is sensible to have more than one solution, because if one idea does not work, you may need to try other strategies. What is essential is to make a note at the end of the meeting of what has been agreed and what is to be done next. Doing it with Leslie with a copy for both parties is good practice, especially because that way Leslie will not be fearful of what you might write about him.

When the strategies have been decided you will want to draft a brief action plan.

One of your responsibilities as Leslie's manager is to monitor progress towards the agreed target. Individual targets are now forming part of appraisal and this whole process could form a part of Leslie's appraisal. Even if he wants to use his subject work for appraisal purposes, the work with you to improve his tutorial skills will contribute towards his ongoing staff development and could be included in his personal profile.

CASE STUDY 5.8

Please will you change our tutor!

A deputation has arrived from one of your Y8 tutor groups. Their request is that Mrs Andrews should not be their form tutor next year. Mrs Andrews has been in the school for a number of years and this is not a new problem. She is conscientious and hard working, yet somehow she is unable to establish a rapport with or even earn respect from her tutor group. Discipline in the group usually begins to break down in year 8, and last time round Mrs Andrews was taken off the group and given a new start with a year-7 form. Now it is happening again. What should you as the year head do this time? What approaches should you take in dealing with this problem? What management style would it be best to adopt? Who should advise you?

What would you, as Mrs Andrews's year head, advise the deputy head, who deals with the allocation of form tutors? The school's general policy is that a tutor goes up the school with his/her form group.

Why Case Study 5.8 is more serious than 5.7

This case study is more serious than the previous one as the teacher is more experienced and the problem is not a new one. It is clear from the case study that it is not the first time that something like this has occurred. Last time round, she was taken off the tutor group and given a new start, so the first issue you have to address is should you do the same?

An instinctive answer to should you move Mrs Andrews is that if it didn't work last time, it does not make sense to use the same strategy again. However, you do not have much information provided in this case study, so it is difficult to know what you should do. The case study is a brief synopsis partly so that you can consider the processes involved and not get bogged down in the personalities. It is also a brief summary because you often have to tackle a problem without knowing enough about it to have solutions readily available, or be sure that you are applying appropriate solutions.

One way to overcome this problem is to use a management model. One that I find very useful in dealing with people problems is to try to apply the problem-solving Approach.

Taking a problem-solving approach

This approach (Figure 5.2) involves tackling a problem in clearly defined stages. It is important not to jump into trying to find solutions to a problem before you have clarified what the problem involves and what your possible avenues for action might be. It is a technique that you can use to depersonalize problems and make them more manageable.

1 Clarifying the problem

If we apply this model to the problem of Mrs Andrews the first step is to try and identify what the problem is about and if there is more than one component. There appear to be two main elements to this problem. The most important is that Mrs Andrews has failed to establish a good relationship with her tutor group. Current symptoms include the pupils' poor behaviour in the tutor period and their request for a change of tutor. The second component is history. What I mean here is that it is not a new problem, but one, which has become compounded by not being solved before.

2 Analysis

The problem lies in the unsatisfactory relationship. What you don't know is why she has failed to bond with her tutor groups.

To analyse this problem successfully you will need a lot more information than you have been given, so you must investigate before you can analyse the data. This should help you to understand the causes and begin to develop possible solutions.

Stages in problem solving

1 Clarification
   - What is the problem?
   - Does it have component parts?
   - What are the current symptoms?

2 Analysis
   - Diagnose the problem
   - Categorize the symptoms
   - Suggest possible causes
   - Consider the viewpoints of the different people concerned

3 Approaches
   - Generate ideas to resolve the problem
   - What are the possible strategies?
   - Who can help with the solutions?

4 Action
   - What can be done in the short term?
   - What can be done in the long term?
   - Specify steps to deal with the problem
   - Decide who is going to monitor progress and agree how this is to be done.

Figure 5.2 Clearly defined stages in problem solving.

You will have to test out some hypotheses

1. It may be that she is a good tutor for year 7 but is much less good with older pupils, in which case she should stay with year 7 and not go up with the group. More likely is that it takes time for the problems to develop and that in year 7 the pupils simply behave better because they are new to the school.
2. It may be that that she is more sympathetic to the needs of older pupils and that giving her a senior or sixth-form group would solve the problem. Again it is more likely that she lacks the skills to deal with the sophisticated problems which arise in the sixth form, and that her reputation as a poor tutor will make the move hard for her.
3. It looks very likely from the information you have so far that this is a case of can't rather than won't. You are told that Mrs Andrews is a conscientious tutor. The deputation is not accusing her of failing to attend to her duties, rather they are saying that they don't value her and that they don't want her to continue as their tutor.
4. There also seems to be an element of the tutor having difficulty in class control. One of the symptoms is the increasingly unruly behaviour of the form. What

you don't know at this stage is whether the problem is specific to the tutor group or more general and applies also to her subject teaching.

5. The question arises as to why the problem has been allowed to go on for so long? She was transferred back to a year-7 group instead of continuing with her form. What support was she given at this stage? Were any strategies applied which would have helped her improve her skills or was she simply moved in the hope that a second chance would solve things? There are issues here about how Mrs Andrews has been managed in the past.

6. One of the major issues at this stage is how Mrs Andrews perceives the problem. Does she know she has a problem? Usually the answer is 'Yes', but the teacher refuses to face it or doesn't know what to do about it. Usually, too, she will not want you to know and will be reluctant to discuss it with you.

Generating strategies

Your investigation of the problem has already generated some ideas about how to proceed. They included:

- moving her to the sixth form;
- keeping her with year 7.

Who can help with this problem?

This is the point when you talk to the people who can help you. Your discussions must be professional, not gossip about another member of staff, and they must be constructive. You are looking for ways to support a member of your team, who appears to be working hard but not succeeding.

You must find out from the previous year head, if s/he is still a member of staff, precisely what happened last time. It is important not to repeat past mistakes. Even if the last team leader is still available, you will also have to discuss the problem with a member of the SMT, probably the person in charge of the pastoral system, but not necessarily. You should talk to the person with the skills to help you handle the problem.

Possible strategy: A deputy acts as a sounding board and helps you to decide your approach and assess how well the strategy is working.

You must also tactfully check with the subject leader whether the problem is purely one of ineffective tutoring or whether Mrs Andrews is also having difficulties with the classes she teaches. If she is having difficulties in both areas, it not only compounds your problem, but partially explains why it has gone on for so long. The tutoring issue has been perceived as the least of her problems, because she has worse problems in the classroom. If so, you definitely need to know what strategies have been applied in the past, and to decide how far you should work in tandem with the subject leader. You do not want to put Mrs Andrews under too much pressure at one time.

Possible strategy: You concentrate on the tutoring issue, but you arrange information sharing with the subject leader so that you know what is going on elsewhere.

The pupils

The other group who can help with this situation are the pupils. If the deputation came from a sensible group, you can talk to them as mature people and they normally respond well to this kind of approach. It is in their interests for the relationship to improve. They should be able to tell you whether there is indiscipline in the whole group or a small part of it or indeed largely provoked by one pupil. A solution could be to move a pupil or pupils. If the deputation is from troublemakers, this will quickly become apparent, and you will also know whether these pupils have a record of complaining about their teachers. If the problem is linked to Mrs Andrew's past reputation, and stories about her which have been passed on by their older brothers or sisters, the pupils could be made to understand that this is unfair to the teacher. Not everyone can be charismatic, and often they do have other qualities. A sensible discussion of her strengths, and your knowledge of what she actually does as form tutor, could help her to be appreciated by the group.

Possible strategy: Ongoing work with these pupils could help the teacher.

4 Action

In the short term

Confront the situation

Once you have the information you need, you must talk to Mrs Andrews. It will quickly leak out that there has been a complaint and it is not fair on the teacher not to know what the situation is. Your interview with Mrs Andrews will not be easy. The better prepared you are, the more successful it is likely to be. Your management style here will need to be firm but not unfriendly. The firmness will be needed initially to establish that not only is there a problem, but that something has to be done about it. It is essential, however, that the teacher's self-esteem is not further eroded. It will be a difficult time for her. Once you have agreed that the problem exists, the approach could become much more collaborative, so that you tackle the problem and draw up your action plan together. Remember to build in a monitoring process at this stage.

Deciding action: Should you move her?

Whether you should move the tutor clearly depends on the answers to the questions posed above. If you have begun to establish a sound working relationship with her, it would probably be better to leave her where she is. You don't want her to have yet another failure.

Communicate your decision to the pupils

Your decision about whether to move Mrs Andrews will have to be communicated to the pupils who came on the deputation. If your work with them is progressing well, they will understand and accept the reasons that you give them. You must be prepared, however, for some protest from the pupils or follow-up letters from their parents. These tend to be sent straight to the headteacher, which is another reason why the SMT needs to be in the picture about how you are dealing with the matter.

In the long term

Implement strategies to support the tutoring

Strategies to support her tutoring would have to be worked out. You will probably need more than one. Which one you use will depend on what was tried last time, and you must be prepared for some failures. You will want the changes and the support to be as unobtrusive as possible. There are plenty of things that you could do. Indeed, when I use this case study (Case Study 5.8) on training seminars for year or house heads, they generally have a lot of ideas to offer. Some ideas could include:

- some tutor meetings devoted to what constitutes good tutoring – sharing of ideas;
- using different tutors to deliver specific parts of the pastoral curriculum;
- some team tutoring;
- individual coaching from you or an appropriate person, probably not a member of the SMT as this could be intimidating for Mrs Andrews;
- use Case Study 5.11 as an example of how good practice or a strong tutor can be used to help others develop their skills;
- target developing her interpersonal skills – her problems centre on forming a relationship with a group;
- build on known strengths. Administratively she appears sound, perhaps she could help another tutor who is weak in dealing with the admin;
- a course on its own is unlikely to help much, but later on perhaps you could send her on a counselling course, which could raise her awareness as well as developing her skills.

It will be difficult for her to change her approach, especially as she is not a new teacher. You should also appreciate that you are unlikely to improve her quickly or develop her out of all recognition. Some improvement, however, is possible. You must support her through what will be a traumatic experience and help her build up her confidence without being dishonest or making statements which you might regret later.

Evaluate progress

How you evaluate progress should have been built into your programme. The simplest method is to check progress together and agree where you think you are. If you design an action plan with a column in which you tick off the targets and date achieved, it should only take a few moments in one of your working sessions together to deal with it. If you have set small and achievable targets, it should be easy enough to know whether you have achieved them. Discussing the progress made and how to consolidate it will take you longer.

If there is major progress ensure that recognition is given (e.g. specific praise from the pastoral deputy or the headteacher, and an input into the teacher's personal record/profile).

The case studies so far have centred on willing tutors. S/he does the job, indeed s/he is sometimes overenthusiastic or, although hardworking, s/he lacks talent. However, one of the problems most consistently raised, when I run training seminars for heads of year or house, is what to do about the reluctant tutor. Case Study 5.9 describes a typical scenario.

CASE STUDY 5.9

The reluctant tutor

Too often when you pop into Tony's tutor group, you find him missing. He does attend your tutor meetings, but tends to bring his marking with him and begins to look at his watch after about half an hour, as if to say, 'Isn't it over yet.' Getting pastoral returns back from Tony is like getting blood out of a stone. What you receive will be late and inaccurate. He spends more time winding you up over this than he does on completing the lists or returning his register to the correct place at the correct time. If you insist that he does the task, he does it so badly that you virtually have to redo it, which often takes you longer than if you had done it yourself. He is scathing about the PSHE programme and clearly does as little as he thinks that he can get away with. He clearly resents the time that he has to spend on what he considers to be a second job, and mutters that in European schools he would not have to do cover or be a form tutor. You are not sure whether this is true, but realize that his whole attitude towards being a tutor is negative and that it is affecting others in your team. You gather from colleagues that he is regarded as a satisfactory subject teacher, but you find him a reluctant and unsatisfactory tutor.

For discussion

- What are the issues involved in this case study?
- What can be done about Tony?
- What advice would you give this pastoral team leader?

WHAT IS THIS PROBLEM ABOUT?

There are two main issues involved in this case study, which is a fairly typical example of the reluctant-tutor problem. First, the tutor is not doing his job properly. Symptoms include:

- late or inaccurate returns;
- he is often not in his classroom with his tutor group during form time.

Second, he has an attitude problem. Symptoms include:

- doing as little as possible;
- doing other jobs during your meeting – rude to you and affects his concentration;
- turning his poor performance into a game against you.

HOW SHOULD YOU DEAL WITH IT?

This kind of problem is very difficult to solve but some general principles apply:

- the longer he is allowed to get away with it, the worse the problem will get. It is also very likely that, because of Tony's attitude, his tutor group is developing bad habits. It is very important to prevent the problem escalating;
- if you do his job for him, he will let you. Don't make a rod for your own back; if registers are involved, there is a legal requirement, which he must fulfil. This could give you a lever;
- developing bad habits is not good for him and could lead to professional disaster;
- do not allow his 'teasing' to irritate you so much that it becomes personal;
- you are entitled to support from your senior managers in dealing with this problem.

SOME STRATEGIES FOR DEALING WITH THE RELUCTANT TUTOR

- In the description of what was happening, the initiative seemed to lie with Tony, and you were having to react. This is a case in which, as the year head, you will want to work out your strategy carefully so that you hold the initiative, not Tony.
- Tony is causing you extra work, and making you feel that it is much easier not to ask him to do things. One of your strategies must therefore be to make him feel that the game is not worth the effort that he is putting into it.
- Your own attitude is crucial. You have to make it clear that you are taking the problem seriously and intend to resolve it. Emphasize that this is not a personal vendetta but a professional issue.
- On the other hand, do keep a sense of perspective. Infuriating as Tony might be, do not allow yourself to become obsessed or depressed by his behaviour or rudeness. Treat it as a little local difficulty, but one which you are going to sort out. Your ability to approach the matter objectively and with detachment will give you an advantage.
- Break the problem down into its component parts and start with what you think you may be able to improve, rather than trying to deal with it all at once. Every little victory will help your morale. It could make sense to start with the

registers. He is seriously out of line if he is not doing this part of his job. Improving his pastoral skills could come later.

- Seek the assistance of your line manager. Working in concert with a member of the senior management does not indicate failure, rather it shows you need a sounding board to help you work out the moves and you actually want senior management to know that you are working hard on this problem.
- All too frequently middle managers, who attend my training seminars, tell me that they have referred the problem, but are not receiving the help to which they are entitled. The advice here is that however difficult it may be, you must persevere. You may prefer to choose your senior manager rather than use your direct line manager.
- Make brief notes on the case including the strategies you are applying for behaviour modification. Later on, it could prove important that you have kept a record of the failures to conform to good practice and the measures you took to rectify the situation.

CASE STUDY 5.10

For action/discussion

The headteacher points out to you that Keiran, one of the younger members of your tutor team, does not wear a tie, although it is in the staff code of practice for this school, and that he looks generally untidy. You consider Keiran to be a promising tutor, who has a lot to offer. You are new in the post and very busy with matters you consider to be much more important than whether Keiran is wearing a tie. You also suspect that Keiran is not going to take kindly to being told he must wear a tie.

For discussion

- What are the issues involved in this case study?
- What advice would you give this year head?

CASE STUDY 5.11

For reflection/discussion

On your team of tutors is Adrian, a very gifted tutor and PSHE specialist. He has created learning experiences for his tutor group that other tutors could only dream about. In order to use his abilities fully, you persuade Adrian to have a year off from being a tutor and instead to act as a tutorial specialist attached to your year-9 team. You have had to convince the SMT that this move will be cost-effective as the school has to use every available body to fill the complement of tutors, and initially there was some reluctance to allow the experiment, but you use all your powers of persuasion. You also have to persuade some members of the team that Adrian is not simply skiving and that there really are advantages for them in having an additional person attached to the team.

Quickly, however, the gamble is seen to pay good dividends. Adrian's work diary is available to the tutors, who book him in advance to work in their classrooms with their students. Having Adrian to deliver a tutor period became so popular that he was booked weeks ahead. The teachers observe Adrian working with the groups and make a note of and evaluate the techniques used on a planning sheet. Occasional tutor INSET sessions are slotted in to enable the team to analyse and discuss the ideas and techniques. For this group of staff the chance to observe good practice enhanced their awareness of possibilities, enabled them to see how an idea might be delivered in practice and increased their understanding of what good tutoring meant. By the end of the year the expertise of the tutor team was substantially increased.

Source: Powell (1997).

For discussion

- Why did this year head have to work hard to persuade the SMT and some team members to support the scheme?
- What did the tutor team gain from the experiment?
- What are the implications of this case study for you as a team leader?

BIBLIOGRAPHY AND FURTHER READING

Powell, R. (1997) *Raising Achievement*, Stafford: Robert Powell Publications.

Chapter 6

Introducing change

Change can be unsettling, threatening and unpredictable. Introducing change can also be an opportunity for creativity and learning …

Sonia Blandford (1997)

CASE STUDY 6.1

For action/discussion

Creating a code of conduct

A year leader describes how her school introduced a code of conduct:

When the SMT [senior management team] was redrafting its whole school behaviour policy, the pastoral deputy put an item onto the year heads' meeting agenda about making the policy meaningful for the pupils. Behaviour in the school was, in Ofsted terms, satisfactory, but we wanted the pupils to take more responsibility for their own behaviour.

At our meeting we spent a long time discussing possible strategies, and finally decided to introduce a code of conduct, which would be largely formulated by the pupils and which would become the last item in the behaviour policy. By the end of the meeting we had decided a procedure and a working timetable. We insisted that we should have sufficient time to do the job properly. The deputy would have liked the code to be in place by half-term, but we persuaded her that it was essential to provide an opportunity for the pupils to have a meaningful exchange of ideas and that it would be counter-productive to rush the initiative. By fixing a time limit of a term for the whole process, however, we ensured that the initiative would move forward at a pace that kept the momentum going. We all had too much experience of talking shops which failed to reach conclusions and settled nothing.

In the school meeting cycle, year-leader meetings were followed 10 days later by year meetings, so we had to decide how to approach the issue with our year teams. We would need to brief them fully about the initiative, but also to win their support for it, because they would be the central figures in managing the dialogue with the pupils. There were some concerns about how this was to be managed as some teams included members who could not be bothered or who would not be able to sell the idea to their tutor group.

At this stage of proceedings, the deputy was extremely supportive. Most importantly she did not underestimate the problem, rather she stressed that a lot of people feel very threatened by any change and we needed to take that factor into account and not take it personally if opposition occurred. She used some good materials, particularly a change-curve diagram, to show us how people tend to react during the introduction of a change. She also responded promptly to our suggestion that the SMT should draft a paper to explain the rationale of the change, producing a clear and concise briefing document, which we could use with our teams when we presented the initiative. She also organized a working lunch in her office, in which she discussed possible approaches with us and suggested strategies we could use to help us win the day. I am sure that this made a difference when we came to hold the team meeting.

In my team very few team members put forward objections. They mainly talked about the difficulties of including yet another item in an already full tutorial programme and there was a suggestion that perhaps we should wait for a more opportune time. Nevertheless, the majority of my team, even those who were worried about time pressures, were actually very supportive and it was agreed by all that there never would be a perfect time and the initiative was too good to postpone. I was particularly pleased that there was some very good discussion of the best way to introduce the initiative to the pupils. I was aware however, one of my team members, Sheila, would need a little private coaching outside the meeting and I worked closely with her to support her through the consultation process. On a bad day she has a tendency to antagonize her group because she is too authoritarian and I was particularly anxious that her discussion session should not become a confrontation.

Deborah, one of the other year heads, however, reported back that she had had a difficult time as Justin, one of her team members, had taken a determinedly negative view. Justin had rubbished the whole initiative and proved himself to be adept at putting spokes in the wheel of the team-making progress. He claimed that the initiative was not a new idea but one that was tried in the distant past and failed then. 'So what makes you think it will succeed now?' he asked witheringly, and argued that there was absolutely no point in introducing a time-consuming initiative, which would only fail in the end. Justin has a reputation for being difficult, and my colleague said that she now realized that he was both a negativist and a talented 'blocker', fitting into at least two of the categories that the deputy had warned us about. Being able to identify the type helped her to deal with this team member with less 'aggro' than might otherwise have been the case. 'I know I avoided traps that I would not have recognized without her advice', she said. Even though another member of the team always opposed the 'blocker' on principle, Deborah was able to prevent a row from breaking out, kept the meeting on task and eventually created enough enthusiasm to carry the day. She was very pleased about this and also with the deputy's recognition of what had been achieved with this difficult team.

It was decided that in tutorial time each tutor group should produce five points or rules for the code and that these should be discussed at year meetings. In this way each year group could formulate its own code. Then we would convene a meeting of the whole school council, which would be devoted wholly to devising a school code from the year codes. The form representatives would attend the school council. Some tutors, and even a member of the SMT, had doubts about the level of discussion that we would get at these council meetings. One of the problems of the school council in the past was that it discussed trivia, especially the content of school lunch menus, or it raised ideas which the previous headteacher promptly rejected, so it was not highly regarded. Nevertheless, it seemed to us that school council was the natural venue to use and that it was important to try it. The fact that it would contribute to our citizenship programme led one of the deputies to give very strong support to calling the year and whole school council meetings.

We had discussed how the sixth form would fit into this. George, the head of sixth, felt strongly that they should discuss the code in their tutor groups and draft a sixth-form code of conduct. It could engender some very good discussions on items such as smoking, he said. He also felt that the form prefects should be involved in helping their forms draw up their suggestions, and he arranged a briefing session led by the head prefect to help the prefects take a constructive line with their forms.

In the event, the pupils reacted very well and some extremely sensible discussions took place at all age groups. For the first time in years it became competitive to be the form representative who went to the school council, so we had to hold elections. As well as producing year and school codes of conduct, the process had an influence on the school rules and some changes were made as a result.

Only on one point was there any real disagreement between pupils and staff, and this was about behaviour on the journey to school. The pupils took the view that once they were off the premises, school rules should not apply. The staff, and particularly the headteacher, who regularly dealt with the complaints about behaviour on the buses or trains, felt strongly, however, that while the pupils were in school uniform, they were representatives of the school and that sensible behaviour on the journey should be included in the code. This disagreement was holding up progress as the headteacher did not want to overrule the pupils, but they were very 'anti' including it. Finally he got the prefects to give a lead to the pupils and used some form time to get them to understand why it mattered. In the end he won the point and the code was finally adopted. Large year codes were printed for the walls of each classroom. The art department sponsored a competition for the best presented illuminated whole-school codes and the winners were displayed prominently in public areas.

Feedback from the tutors and the pupils indicated that the process was felt to be valuable both because so many people had been involved and because the 'powers that be' had been prepared to listen to suggestions. This was felt to be an important change in the culture of the school. It was more difficult, of course, to assess the effect on behaviour especially as discipline was not a major issue. We monitored pupil behaviour for the rest of the academic year. As a group of year heads we came to the view that in a number of situations the pupils did behave more sensibly than they might have done previously, and that behaviour on the corridors and at the bus stop appeared to have improved. We could not prove that this was a direct effect of the code of conduct, but overall we were pleased.

The code had been high profile and we were concerned that with the passing of time the *effect would decrease, so at a year heads' meeting, towards the end of the year, we discussed what we should do to keep the momentum going. We felt that the consultation sessions had been essential to the success of the initiative and that we should build into our tutorial programme a regular session in which the pupils were not only reminded of the code, but were also given an opportunity to make modifications if they wished. One suggestion that was acted upon was that the assembly cycle could be used effectively to reinforce the code, although it was felt that a pupil-led assembly would have more impact that a monologue delivered by the headteacher.*

In the 3 years since then, the code of conduct has become firmly enmeshed in the school culture. In a recent evaluation with the pupils, many said that they valued it. The major effect for the school was a real sea change in our willingness to consult the pupils about important matters and to take note of their views. It has given a new lease of life to the school council, which now meets to discuss important issues in the certainty that it can influence decisions.

For discussion

What are the lessons of this case study for you as a pastoral manager?

The introduction of a code of conduct into the school was effective for a number of reasons. These included:

1. thorough planning and review;
2. the change was not rushed – it was done over a term and the stages assimilated;
3. the initiative was carefully structured – with a clear timetable of development;
4. it was school specific – designed to fit a need;
5. the difficulties were not underestimated;
6. the managers were given some training in how to present and handle the change;
7. the SMT gave strong support and good leadership;
8. consultative and collaborative – it was not simply a top-down initiative, a lot of people were involved;
9. consultation was real – people could see that good suggestions were adopted;
10. an evaluation process was built in and used.

1 Thorough planning and review

The planning of this initiative was well handled. Although it was not all planned at the beginning, there were regular sessions in which progress was reviewed and thought was given to what would be needed at the next stage of the initiative.

2 The change was not rushed

One of the biggest traps is ... the failure of organisational leaders to resist the temptation to rush through the planning process to get to the action stage ...
(Beckhard and Harris 1977)

It is very understandable that managers want to get an important initiative in place as fast as possible. In this case, however, the middle managers very sensibly resisted the desire of the SMT to complete the whole initiative in half a term. Cutting corners and skimping on the time needed to get a change right can be a recipe for disaster. Change has two aspects – content and process. Taking a term indicated the importance placed on getting the process right as well as the content. It also made it easier for the school to assimilate the change.

3   The initiative was carefully structured

The timetable for change was worked out and adhered to. It fitted into the meeting cycle and provided a framework for development. A term gave sufficient time for discussion, yet kept the pace brisk. Meetings were set targets (e.g. produce five points for the code), and representatives had to report back to their forms. All this helped prevent them from declining into talking shops.

4   It was school specific – designed to fit a need

Part of the reason why this initiative met with a good reception was that people could see its purpose. They appreciated that this was neither yet another externally imposed initiative, nor the whim of a senior manager, but a sensible idea that could help the school to achieve one of its aims. It was a straightforward project (a small initiative), yet it involved a great many people and, in the end, it affected the culture of the school – this, of course, was a major change.

5   The difficulties were not underestimated

It is very tempting when you are enthused about a particular project to underestimate the problems which might arise, but change is always difficult to introduce. It is not merely that inevitably there will be hitches, some of which you cannot anticipate, but that many people are innately conservative and find any change threatening. It is much better for you to anticipate possible problems and have strategies to hand to help you deal with them, than to have to firefight, dealing with one crisis after another. In this way you are a proactive manager rather than a reactive one.

6   The managers were given some training in how to present and handle the change

A clear briefing paper, which they receive in advance of the meeting, is usually a good way of helping people assimilate change. This way there is less of the surprise element and less threat. If everyone receives the same information, it helps avoid suspicion either that you have favourites or that it is all a plot.

The training in handling difficult team members was particularly valuable in this instance because the year leaders were more confident in dealing with the difficulties than they might have been otherwise.

7 The SMT gave good leadership

If an initiative is simply top led, there is little that the middle managers can do to influence it and in such circumstances you tend to feel 'done to'. Certainly you don't regard it in the same way as when you have ownership of the scheme. In this case the SMT led the initiative very well. The original initiative came from the SMT, but although they provided the support and pressure necessary to keep it going, they resisted the tendency to over-control it and in the end shared the ownership. It is usually the case that if the head or SMT back an initiative, it has a better chance of success than if they are not involved or interested. It was clear to everyone in this school that the SMT wanted this initiative to succeed.

The pastoral deputy provided particularly good leadership. She was approachable and helpful. At all stages of this development, the middle managers could discuss problems or issues with her either as a group or on an individual basis. They found her suggestions helpful and acted on them.

She was responsive to their needs. Most noticeably she drafted the briefing paper for the middle managers to use with their teams. Although it might have been better for them to have had some input into this document, it saved them time and ensured that all the teams were given the same basic information. She also provided some very useful training in how to cope with the more difficult members of their teams.

8 There was very thorough consultation at all levels

Although the scheme originated from the senior management, it actually provided everyone with the opportunity to give their view and a variety of forums for discussion. This made people feel valued and involved.

9 Consultation was real

People could see that good suggestions were adopted.

10 An evaluation process built in and used

For discussion

How does the introduction of the code of conduct match against the checklist of factors, which have been found to influence effective management of change?

- Successful change requires support and pressure.
- Each change has two components – content and process.
- Headteachers have the most important role in managing change.
- Change needs to be communicated fully to those involved.
- Teachers need to be convinced of the need for change.
- Individual teachers need to take ownership of the change.
- Effective change needs clear plans and procedures.

- Moving towards small concrete goals works better than setting vast targets, no matter how desirable.
- Each stage needs to be assimilated for the next to succeed.
- Past experience of successful/unsuccessful change influences attitudes and expectations.
- Change works best in an organization which has been trained to accept change.

Source: Nathan (1991).

For discussion:

1. How does the introduction of the code of conduct match against the checklist?
2. You may wish to compare the introduction of this initiative with the introduction of the after-school clubs for year 7 described in Chapter 9. What are the common features of managing these two initiatives?

Bibliography and further reading

Beckhard and Harris (1977) *Organisational Transition, Managing Complex Change*,
Blandford, S. (1997) *Middle Management in Schools*, London: Pitman Publishing.
Nathan, M. (1991) *Senior Management in Schools, A Survival Guide*, Oxford: Blackwell.

Chapter 7

Dealing with parents

INTRODUCTION

Your role as a pastoral leader ensures that you deal with a lot of 'outsiders'. You see parents more than anyone else in the school. This means that, as a year head, you can affect the interaction between home and school more than any other manager. There is also a public-relations component of your management role and you will need to think about how you should handle it.

I MANAGING AN EVENT

What are the most important management skills you need for this component of your role?

- Organizational skills – there is a lot of organization involved in managing an event.
- Communications skills – you must provide clear information in a user-friendly way.
- Interpersonal skills – you need to get a positive response from parents and staff.

What kind of events are you likely to have to manage?

The main event for which you are likely to be responsible is the parents' evening for your year group, when parents come into school to gather information about how their child is progressing. Other events include sessions to provide parents with information about specific parts of their curriculum (e.g. new-parents' evenings, options evenings, Personal, Social and Health Education [PSHE] sessions, speakers on specific topics, careers events, etc.).

Organizing a pupil-progress meeting

Most schools provide one annual session for each year group to meet the teachers specifically to discuss their child's progress. Occasionally, especially at year 9, two sessions are provided. At a pupil-progress meeting, what matters to the school is that the parents of the pupils attend and that there is a productive dialogue between the school and the parents. What matters to the parents is that they can acquire the information that they need about the progress of their child and constructive advice about how to rectify any problems, which may be arising.

Some guidelines for managing a parents' evening

These guidelines are intended to help new year/house heads manage their first parents' meeting, but they could also serve as a benchmark against which more experienced middle managers can check their own practice. They can be adapted for other kinds of meetings.

Start early

You need about 4 weeks to get the parents' evening set up. This doesn't mean that you work non-stop for 4 weeks, but that you must allow sufficient time for each stage and that you can preempt or deal with problems as they arise. If you want to book the Careers Officer to attend, you should see that s/he has the school calendar at least a term ahead and that the date is in his/her diary. Confirm her availability when you start to make the arrangements.

Check that all the staff are available

Make an alphabetical list of the staff needed for the evening and put the list up on the appropriate board in the staffroom about a month before the meeting. Allow a week for them to tick that they can come, and then check those who haven't signed up. Find out whether they have not noticed the list or simply not got around to signing it or whether there is a real problem.

If a member of staff is not going to be available, you should see the head of the subject department to arrange a facility for the parents to see the head of department. The teacher should do this him/herself, but you cannot rely on this happening, so you should take the initiative. The teacher concerned must, however, leave comments about the pupils and to have explained them to the head of department (HoD), so that s/he can talk to the parents.

Will there be an appointments system?

Schools vary about using an appointments system. Partly this depends on the normal turnout and partly the ethos of the school. Some schools have a mixed system because the needs of different year groups fit different systems. Increasingly, however, schools do seem to be moving to an appointments system, because parents dislike queuing for long periods. If you decide to operate an appointments system make sure that it delivers your objectives. If after the meeting you receive a crop of letters or phone calls grumbling about the appointments system, you will know that you haven't quite got it right yet.

Most schools involve the pupils in arranging the appointments for their parents. What you should guard against here is that they may only arrange appointments for their good subjects, so start by getting the teachers to list the parents that they really want to see and then get the pupils to fill in the gaps. Be realistic about the time slots, especially if you are using more than one room or hall for the meeting and parents have to go from one room to another. An appointment every 5 minutes tends to be too short, 10-minute gaps work better.

At this stage, check which staff have more than one teaching group in the year, and start to make a contingency plan to help those who, for example, teach three sets of Y9 modern languages (i.e. ca. ninety pupils) and who will not be able to see ninety sets of parents. Even if some staff start their appointments earlier than other teachers, there will still be parents who can't be fitted in. As a manager your aim is to avoid disappointing parents. If you are new to the post, check what the school normally does in these circumstances and evaluate whether the existing system is satisfactory.

Liaise with caretaker and check back before the meeting

Being on good terms with the caretaker in the period up to and including the meeting is vital. The caretaker should arrange the room for you including putting out the staff desks, and clearing them away afterwards. Give him/her a copy of the seating plan well in advance and discuss through any potential difficulties. This means that you should be aware of any constraints of access to the required area and whether, for example, the hall is needed for assembly first thing next morning. Check with an experienced year head what the caretaker is normally expected to do, because if you are inexperienced, s/he may try to do less than usual and you could find yourself having to persuade pupils or parents to move desks or chairs at the end of the meeting. This should not be necessary!

Publish template of seating plan

In the week of the meeting publish, usually on the staffroom notice board, the template of the seating arrangements. This lets the teachers know where they will be sitting for the evening, which sometimes affects the arrangements that they make with individual parents.

On the night see that a large copy of the seating plan is posted where all parents can refer to it as they arrive. It is normally useful to have some duplicated A4 copies of the seating plan available, and some schools provide each parent with a copy of the seating plan and list of the teachers.

You may have total freedom in how you arrange the seating, or you may have to rotate staff according to a school programme to avoid grumbles about the same department getting the worst places every time, so check if there is an agreed procedure. In some schools the headteacher welcomes the parents at the beginning or makes a brief input halfway through. Check what usually happens at your school and include information about this on the plan.

Check whether all the parents are coming

In the week of the meeting ask for feedback from the tutors about who is coming. Usually this is done on a form list and it shows up immediately which parents haven't responded or can't come.

Contact parents who can't come

When you find that parents whom staff would very much like to see are listed as not attending, check if they have given a good reason for their non-attendance; a few phone calls home at this stage could be useful. Not only will it help your public relations, it will also indicate to the pupil and his/her parents that you are aware that they are not coming. It gives you an opportunity for a brief word with parents who may not need to come in at all, but who are likely to be pleased to be given the opportunity for a short chat and the reassurance that everything is OK. If the initiative comes from you, it helps avoid the *'Please can we come in on Wednesday afternoon and see all of Bobby's teachers'* that appears in Case Study 7.1. In some cases you will have to phone the parents to find out whether they actually received the letter of invitation. In a small number of cases you will want to take the initiative in fixing an appointment at another time.

Brief the staff about possible problems

If the school has a regular slot to give information (e.g. a morning briefing session) it is a good idea to book the slot a day or so in advance of the meeting. This is the time to alert the staff about those parents who can't come so they don't spend a lot of time waiting for someone who has made it quite clear that s/he will not be present, and for you to say what you are doing about contacting parents who should be seen but are not coming. Sometimes you have to warn staff about possible troublemakers. The usual way to do this is to make a list of those who may become argumentative and should be immediately sent on to see you or a member of the senior management team (SMT).

Be available and be prepared to troubleshoot

On the night do not overload yourself with appointments, especially those which would be better done on another occasion. As a subject teacher you will have a list of whom you must see, but try to keep it short, as you are the section manager, and you should be available to see parents who encounter unexpected difficulties and you may have to troubleshoot.

Evaluate afterwards

After the meeting it is useful to check (e.g. at another briefing session) how the staff perceived the evening. This will help you pick up on problems which should have come your way, but haven't. It will also clarify whether the organization of the evening was satisfactory. Keep your record of the evening on file or disc, not just as a guide for next time but because sometimes you have to refer to it.

Quite frequently teachers find that, at other events, parents will approach them for additional information or to raise issues about their child's progress. Brief your team on how to handle these inquiries appropriately.

2 DEALING WITH PARENTS

Some case studies: for action/discussion

After the parents' meeting you receive a series of letters and a few phone calls from parents of pupils in your year group. Mainly, Case Studies 7.1–7.4 are typical of the kind of missive you receive, one or two are more complex.

If you want to treat these case studies as ones for discussion do not read the analysis until after you have talked through each problem.

For action/discussion: analyse the issues and suggest appropriate responses.

CASE STUDY 7.1

We couldn't come ...

We were unable to attend the recent parents' meeting, but would like to meet Bobby's teachers to discuss his progress. Please will you arrange this for us. A Wednesday afternoon would be convenient ...

When I use this case study with groups of heads of year or house, it is always greeted with a wry laugh. It is the absolutely classic letter from a set of parents and you can expect to receive many like this. There is no right answer, of course, because schools vary enormously in their practice in regard to parents, but there are some general principles that you can apply which will be influenced by the culture and practice prevailing in your own school.

Very few schools would be able, or indeed willing, to release all of Bobby's teachers, even one at a time, to meet his parents on a Wednesday afternoon. Wednesday afternoon might be convenient for the parents, but the teachers will be timetabled and most will not be free. A minority of schools would make a point of providing release for each teacher to see Bobby's parents, say for 10 minutes each, but this is not the usual response. Rather the majority will send round a form, often nicknamed 'the round robin', which asks each subject teacher to comment on Bobby's current performance.

If progress is universally good, a phone call home to tell the parents that all is going very well could surface, although you would want to offer the opportunity for Bobby's parents to come in for a discussion with the form tutor if they so desire. In this case it can be left to them to decide. If there are some areas of concern, then you will certainly want to book an appointment with the parents to see you or the tutor. Which of you will front the interview will depend on the procedure operated by the school.

Sometimes the 'round robin' will produce comments which you feel should lead to a discussion between the teacher and the parents or the parents, will want to talk to a particular teacher. In this case you will need to make the necessary arrangements for a short meeting. We can't tell from Case Study 7.1 whether Wednesday afternoon is really the only time that Bobby's parents can come into school or whether it is essential that they both come. You will have to negotiate the time and, if there are real difficulties, go and see the member of staff responsible for cover and come to a sensible arrangement.

It has been my experience that however you cycle parents' meetings, there will be problems for some parents in being able to attend. Normally you will collate returns for a parents' meeting beforehand and will know roughly how many parents will not be attending. In some cases you will ring the parents at that stage and check, if the return does not indicate this, why the parents can't attend, whether they want information about their child's progress and, if so, in what form. If you get a lot of Bobby letters after the meeting, you may have to hold some sort of session for these parents. A lot will depend on why this has happened. One 'meeting' that often needs a second smaller session is the one for new parents held in the summer term after the pupils have been allocated their new schools, and provision for this may have to be made in the term's timetable, but perhaps with some flexibility.

CASE STUDY 7.2

You must take immediate action to deal with this problem ...

At the parents' meeting Miss Scott said that Jane seemed to be rather isolated within the form. Jane is still new and, at the start of term, we hoped that she would settle in and any problem would disappear, or that you, as her form teacher, would take any necessary steps to deal with it. We are therefore disappointed to find that far from any improvement, the situation appears to have worsened. Jane arrived home yesterday in a very distressed state, because there were two lessons, Games and English, in which she was left without a partner. We want the matter investigated forthwith and expect that you will take action to ensure that Jane will experience no further problems ...

This problem is more serious than the previous one, but it too contains some classic features. One of them is 'Miss Scott said ...' (i.e. a parent quotes back at you something a member of staff is supposed to have said to which the parent has taken exception). You usually have no way of knowing precisely what was said, because you were not present at the encounter. In this case my advice would not be to allow yourself to get bogged down in trying to find out what was actually said. The real problem is about how a pupil is integrating into the form, not about what Miss Scott may or may not have said. You will want to consult Miss Scott in her capacity as Jane's form tutor. She also needs to be informed that the problem appears to be escalating. You have to deal with this letter personally not just because it is addressed to you, but because the form tutor has become one of the parties to the dispute.

Another classic feature is the demand that you take action immediately to rectify the situation. As a year or house head, you must expect to receive a lot of aggressively expressed 'What are *you* going to do about it?' letters and you must resist the temptation to write back in aggressive terms denying your responsibility. You will want to respond either to inform the parents that you are investigating the situation and will let them know as soon as possible what action you are taking and stressing that to act precipitately could make matters worse for Jane, or you could fix a meeting with them. My own preference would be to phone to say that you have the matter in hand and to see Jane as soon as possible.

What actually matters here is the pupil, Jane, and your first step must be to see Jane and find out how she views the situation. Your counselling and listening skills will be needed to encourage her to talk honestly to you. Does she think she has a problem and just how serious is it? What exactly happened in those lessons yesterday, and is she regularly left without a partner – a situation which can be very embarrassing for a teenager. You will have to discover whether Miss Scott's comment at the parents' meeting made Jane's parents' get the situation out of proportion, whether the problem has been steadily getting worse over term and what Jane thinks should happen next.

The demand for immediate action is, of course, totally unreasonable. You cannot be expected to solve the problem immediately, especially if you are dealing with a very unhappy lonely child. What they are really saying, however, is that they want you to do something to help their daughter and this is not unreasonable. Even if the problem is less serious than Jane's parents believe, as her year or house head you would want to do your best for Jane.

There are a number of ways in which you can improve the situation for her. While you cannot find permanent friends for Jane, you could have a quiet word with some of the more sensible members of the form to ensure that she is not left isolated, especially when the form has to take partners or get into groups. Talking to these pupils will also help you to discover how others perceive Jane and what they think has been happening and whether she rejects overtures.

You can also involve her teachers in helping Jane. For example, a general reminder to staff about ensuring that group or pair work does not leave any pupils without partners should help without identifying Jane as a pupil in distress.

Discuss the situation with Miss Scott. You have two matters to deal with here. Most importantly, as Jane's tutor Miss Scott will have watched how Jane is integrating into the form and will have a view about the problem. Listen carefully to what she has to say, then compare her perception of the problem with what you are learning from the members of the form and from Jane herself. You must judge how similar or different the picture is and form your own assessment of the nature and difficulty of the problem. It is essential to reach an understanding with Miss Scott, because she will have to monitor what is happening on a day-to-day basis and feed back to you on progress.

You also have to help Miss Scott mend her fences with Jane's parents. Avoid any blame, and get both sides to concentrate on working together to help the girl. If the tutor's confidence has been affected, you may need to reassure her. There could be a case for including a new target for Miss Scott – improving how she handles difficult parents at progress meetings.

Jane will probably need some counselling in order to identify and confront the problem and to find a way to improve her situation. Very few schools can afford to have even part-time counsellors, so you are likely to have to deal with this personally, but if there is a member of staff to whom she is beginning to relate well, this person could be asked to help Jane. Counselling pupils is discussed in Chapter 9.

CASE STUDY 7.3

You have got it wrong

At the beginning of the year you issued all your tutors with a list of all the pupils who should receive two sets of documents and clear instructions about what to do. Nevertheless something appears to have gone wrong . . .

. . . I heard from a friend yesterday that a progress meeting for Tommy's form took place a couple of weeks ago. When he joined the school last year, I requested that, as we are divorcing, I should be informed of such events separately from Tommy's mother. Now I find that I have missed a meeting, which could have given me information about Tommy's progress. I am particularly upset as year 9 is such an important year for him and critical decisions have to be made. Please will you ensure that in future I am informed about all school functions which I should attend, and let me know when it would be convenient for me to come into school to discuss Tommy's progress with you and/or the relevant teachers . . .

Something has clearly gone wrong here and the situation must be rectified immediately. If the school has made a mistake or handled a situation badly, it is important to admit the mistake and apologize promptly. As long as the divorce gave the father right of access including, receiving his own copy of documentation and attending school functions and progress meetings, you will have to apologize, and try to find out why the information was not sent. The most likely reason, of course, is human error – someone forgot. There is no point in recriminations, but you should firmly remind the tutor and the office that in future they must ensure that two sets are sent. Then you should make an effort to rectify the situation by sending him a copy of any information that he should have received that term, including a list of school functions and events. He may not be allowed to see his son frequently. It is likely that he will *be anxious* about whether the divorce is having an adverse effect on Tommy's progress; so, if possible, offer to see Tommy's father at a time convenient to you both and provide the information he is seeking.

Sometimes a problem emerges at a parents' meeting

You hope that a parents' meeting will not bring unpleasant surprises. Case Study 7.4 explores what happens if a teacher keeps a problem to himself, but uses the parents' meeting to try to put pressure on the pupils through their parents.

CASE STUDY 7.4

'He said that Kevin is a sloth ...'

It is the morning after the parents' meeting. The phone rings. It is Kevin's mother. She is very distressed. *Last night at the parents' evening*, she says, '*I was very pleased that the teachers were so positive about Kevin. He seemed to be working really well and making good progress. Then, almost at the end I saw the science teacher, Mr Fielding. He has only taught Kevin since the beginning of term, but he was full of complaints both about Kevin and the whole form. Apparently they all behave badly in class and are inattentive and chatty. Their standard of work is not what it should be and homework is late and poorly presented. The list seemed endless. Mr Fielding described Kevin as a 'sloth', who mucks about all the time and has to be pressurized to work. I didn't recognize Kevin, who spends hours on his homework. I am very upset, because science is such an important subject and I am not quite sure what to say to Kevin. I thought I'd have a word with you first ...*'

Mr Fielding is new to the school and you do not know him well, but you were under the impression that he is competent. The class does not have a reputation for bad behaviour and Kevin appears to be a capable and co-operative pupil, so you are surprised. This is clearly an incident in which you have to say to the parent, 'Leave it with me for the time being, while I investigate,' as you need to consult Mr Fielding as quickly as possible. The parent is anxious and distressed, so you must fix a time in which you will report back and this should not be more than a day or so after the initial inquiry.

When you see Mr Fielding, he reiterates his complaints about the form, whose behaviour and concentration span he feels leaves much to be desired. Kevin, he says, is one of a group of idle and disruptive boys, who prevent the form from making progress. Surprised, you ask first why he hasn't mentioned this to you before and especially before the parents' meeting, and second you want to know if he has spoken to his head of department and what measures are being taken to deal with the problem. The answers to these questions are not satisfactory. Mr Fielding says he had not mentioned it to you because the problem had been building up slowly and he had thought that as the pupils got to know him the behaviour in the form would improve. For the same reason he has not as yet discussed it with his head of department.

You manoeuvre a meeting in the playground with Kevin and one of Kevin's close friends, Terry, also a reasonable pupil, and have a quiet word about things in general, carefully bringing science into the conversation. Both boys become a bit sheepish. No, they say, science isn't one of their favourite subjects this term. They don't want to say more, but eventually they admit that science has become a lesson in which you 'muck around'. You whisk them into your office to investigate further. Their version of things is that they find it difficult to follow Mr Fielding's explanations, and that he doesn't encourage questions or listen to them. Science is boring now, they claim and you don't learn anything, so people don't attend; there has been some bad behaviour, and one or two people, not them of course, have skipped the lesson altogether. Although they feel that what is happening in science isn't really their fault, but the teacher's, they know that they are not working properly, and they are actually a bit worried about this as Y9 is a crucial year for them. Terry even admits that he has been thinking about asking his parents to get him a coach for science.

All this is very worrying. Your immediate strategy is to give them the traditional year head's pep talk about the importance of working hard in all lessons and tell them that you will be keeping a personal eye on how they behave in science.

In the longer term you have a problem on your hands. The first thing that you have to find out is whether this is a subject-specific problem or whether the behaviour of the group is deteriorating in other areas. You will have to see the form tutor and check whether there are beginning to be problems with this group in any other lessons. The tutor is surprised. His impression is that the form is working well.

It looks as if the problem is related to one teacher, and that it is subject specific. This suggests that it is not essentially a pastoral problem and you must beware of over-stepping boundaries. To deal with the problem, you must liaise with the head of department and bring her up to date with what has happened as quickly and as professionally as possible. In most schools, it is the head of department who is re-sponsible for behaviour in the classroom. Mr Fielding, for reasons you could guess, has not admitted to the head of department that he is experiencing difficulties with a Y9 group. You need to know what the head of department knows or has guessed about the situation, and if Mr Fielding has been experiencing difficulties with any other group.

Sally, the head of department, admits that she is becoming concerned about Mr Fielding. The one lesson that she observed earlier in the term was satisfactory, but in the last week or two, however, she had begun to suspect that all was not well. So far she has not been able to persuade Mr Fielding to confide in her. He has kept insisting that everything was OK. Now it is clear that he needs help and it is her job, not yours, to provide it.

Your role is to monitor the behaviour of the form so that they conform to an acceptable standard. Your conversation with Kevin and Terry indicated, for example, that some pupils are truanting in this subject. Absence from lessons adversely affects pupil progress, so checking on lesson attendance for Y9 science is perfectly in order. Indeed, it will indicate to the form that you know what is going on and could make them anxious to avoid trouble. This could help Mr Fielding re-establish his control over the group.

You must report back to and reassure Kevin's mother. As measures to help Mr Fielding improve his relationship with this class are in process, you don't want to say anything which could make things difficult for the teacher. You will have to admit that there has been a problem. Make it clear, however, that measures are being taken to put things right. You can also reassure her that, although Kevin's recent progress in science was not quite as good as it should have been, he has agreed to work harder and you will be monitoring the situation. There remains the issue of what Kevin's mother should say to Kevin, who does not know that she has spoken to you. In this case, if she doesn't want to tell him, Kevin need not know that his mother rang the school. It could be better simply for her to tell him that his least favourable report was for science and see what Kevin has to say.

Dealing with a complaint from a parent

Complaints from parents arise when:

- they feel that the school has got things wrong;
- their child is not succeeding for some reason;
- a teacher is victimizing their child.

Sometimes the complaint will be about how you handled things and you will need to review your own approach. More often it will involve at least one other teacher and you will have to handle the situation extremely sensitively. Frequently a complaint goes straight to the headteacher and is handed on for your comments on the situation or for you to deal with before the reply, which you may have to draft for the head, goes out under the headteacher's name. The case studies which follow provide some examples of these situations and offer strategies which you could adopt.

CASE STUDY 7.5

I totally disapprove!

Some of your year group acted as guides for a recent new intake session in which families of potential pupils visited the school. A senior teacher organized the session, but you were asked to provide volunteers. After the session an incensed parent rang you. *'My daughter was told to lie!'* she said angrily. *'I expect the school to teach young people that honesty should be a guiding principle. Sarah was instructed to be "economical with the truth" and I totally disapprove!'*

When you investigate, you discover that Sarah had asked the teacher what she should say if she was asked about her journey to school. The journey to school is an issue because the school is highly subscribed and there are a number of pupils who use more than one form of transport to school. In Sarah's case, she has a difficult journey as her family has moved since she joined the school, but she did not want to change schools.

Complaints quite frequently arise because a child reports home something that is really innocuous, but to which the parents, who receive a partial picture of what happened, take exception. This complaint is less serious than some the school might have to face, but you are in a difficult position because the organizer is actually senior to you, and one strategy could be to pass the problem straight to the person concerned to make his own peace with the parent.

It might be better, however, for you to defuse the situation on behalf of the teacher. The parent wants to shout at someone and needs to give vent to his/her feeling of anger. Sometimes it is easier for the school if the person dealing with the angry phone call isn't the guilty party, because then you can get the parent to agree that they shouldn't be shouting at you because it clearly wasn't your fault. If the anger is aimed at you personally, it is very important to remain calm and not allow the interview to deteriorate into a slanging match.

Never rush an interview with an angry parent. Show that you are visibly prepared to give time and listen to what is said; then, after a while, the parent tends to calm down and becomes much more reasonable. Attentive listening is an important skill in dealing with upset or angry parents. Letting an angry parent harangue you is not a very pleasant experience, but it clears the air and then usually the parent is apologetic for having lost control and you are able to move the discussion on. Guidelines for handling aggression are given below.

Obviously, as in all these incidents, you will have to check what was actually said but your strategy will be to clarify the school's real objective in this instance. Your stance is that whatever words he might have used, Mr Wells did not intend Sarah to lie on behalf of the school. Do not attempt to defend the actual phrase, particularly if you do not know if it was the phrase used, or only the idea. Even Mr Wells may not remember this accurately. You may have to concede that his choice of terminology was unfortunate because the phrase is associated with politicians, some of whom have an unsavoury reputation.

What you want to concentrate on is redefining the problem and look for areas of agreement. The issue is really about giving potential pupils a fair view of the school. Pupils are used as guides because what they say about the school will carry conviction and because it encourages them to take responsibility. It is not in your interest to encourage pupils to tell lies about the school, because it would quickly become obvious if they are not telling the truth. Every school has advantages and disadvantages. In this case it is probably fair to say that the advantages vastly outweigh the disadvantages. It is actually important for the parents to be aware of any difficulties so that they can make their decision in the full knowledge of the facts.

You can agree that the journey is a problem for some pupils, nevertheless the school is a very popular choice for parents, many of whom who are prepared to let their sons and daughters travel considerable distances. Emphasizing that what the school had to offer more than compensates for any problems with travel and that learning to cope with the journey to work is part of growing up, is not lying, nor even being economical with the truth. Indeed, you could point out that Sarah valued being a member of the school enough for her to choose not to change schools to make her own journey to school much easier. Suggest that next time she acts as a guide she could tell potential parents this.

This isn't a case in which a lot of action has to be taken. The parent needs to be reassured that the school is not giving out messages to pupils to tell untruths in order to sell the school to potential parents. In other situations you may need to offer to monitor whether there has been an improvement.

The main strategies which emerge from Case Study 7.5 could be used in dealing with any difficult interview. They are:

- remain calm;
- listen attentively;
- be responsive;
- allow the parent to have his/her say;
- deflect the aggression;

- concentrate on identifying the real issues, not on what words s/he might have said;
- consult others where necessary;
- move the situation forward by offering some solutions;
- include the parent in working out the solution;
- offer to monitor the situation if necessary.

Case studies: for action

CASE STUDY 7.6

'I should have been told!'

Mrs Matcham is vociferous in her complaint. She had had a bad time at the parents' evening. Cindy's efforts are poor and her progress this term does not match her ability or her potential. Mrs Matcham is clearly very worried. She is not arguing about Cindy's lack of effort. Mrs Matcham has not seen Cindy do much homework recently, but her daughter has said either that she had done it at lunch time or that not much had been set that day. She has recently acquired her first boyfriend and her mother appreciated that this could have affected her concentration in class and on her homework. 'They do spend a lot of time on the phone to each other, but I insist that she spends at least an hour on her work when she gets home and I only allow her to go out with him at weekends.' Her complaint is that if Cindy's work is deteriorating, she, as Cindy's parent, should have been told much sooner and not left to find it out at the parents' meeting. To her mind the school was failing in its duty to her daughter and to her as a parent.

Although you led a session in the last staff meeting before the progress meeting, which was designed to pick up new problems of this sort as well as checking the progress of ongoing ones, no one amongst the teaching staff has mentioned Cindy's performance to you. If you have the right procedures in place, there should be no surprises, but sometimes there are.

For action/discussion

- How should you answer Mrs Matcham (1) immediately, (2) in the longer term?
- What should you do about the problem?

What is your role in dealing with a serious complaint?

Case Study 7.7 has some similarities to the parent who is distressed at hearing her son described as a sloth, but it is a more difficult and extreme example. It is a complaint about a teacher, who is a head of a large department. Use the analysis of the earlier examples and the guidelines provided above to analyse and resolve this problem.

CASE STUDY 7.7

A parent arrives without an appointment

Mr Black has arrived at your office at 8 a.m. He is both angry and upset. 'You have got to do something about Mr. Treaves!' he exclaims. 'This teacher is harassing my daughter.' When you calm him down enough to get him to tell you what has happened to put him in this state, the following story emerges.

Elisabeth, who is in 10B, has been very withdrawn and rather tearful lately. Something was clearly distressing her. She began to have nightmares, which had not occurred since she was a small child, but the Blacks could not get her to say what was wrong. Elisabeth kept insisting that nothing was the matter. Yesterday when she came home from school she was in an extremely distressed state. At first she would not say what it was, then she asked tentatively if we'd mind if she gave up French. That set alarm bells ringing and Mrs Black probed gently, but persistently, and eventually persuaded Elisabeth her to tell her what was upsetting her so badly. It appears that the Head of Modern Languages is giving Elisabeth a really bad time. He is extremely sarcastic, belittling her and ridiculing her efforts, persistently targeting every small mistake until Elisabeth becomes so upset that she can't do anything right. Yesterday he appears to have excelled himself. He compared her efforts with the worst work of a 5-year-old, reduced Elisabeth to tears in front of the class, set her additional work and gave her some kind of ultimatum about giving it in today. It was not French homework last night and Mr Black had refused to allow Elisabeth to do the work, insisting that she did the subjects that were on the homework timetable for Wednesday evening.

'She seemed to be terrified of what might happen if she did not do these tasks, so I said that when the other work was completed she could have a go. She did try, but by that time she was almost asleep; and anyway I can't believe that in the state she was in she would produce anything worth having. I appreciate that she may not be the top pupil in the set, but she is a conscientious girl and spends hours on her homework. When I said that I would have a word with the school, it seemed to terrify her even more and she implored me not to come. That's partly why I came so early. I thought that you were the best person to consult because you are Elisabeth's Head of Year, know her well and have helped her in the past. I will not tolerate my daughter being treated like this! Something should be done about Mr Treaves. I know that Mr Treaves has a reputation for insisting on high standards, but being a teacher does not give you the right to bully pupils . . .'

For discussion

- What are the issues in this case study?
- What is your role in dealing with a complaint involving a senior member of staff?
- Who should help or support you in managing this problem?
- What support can you give the pupil?
- How do you deal with the angry and distressed parent?

One of the issues you will have to consider in Case Study 7.7 is that the complaint is about how a subject teacher is behaving in his classroom. This is outside your area of responsibility and attempting to deal with it could involve you in boundary disputes. This is not buck-passing. If the charge of harassing a pupil is made against one of your tutors, it is your responsibility, although I would still advise you not to try and deal with it on your own, but to consult senior management because of the seriousness of the charge being made. In this case the complaint is about a member of staff who is actually senior to you. Using all the strategies suggested in the previous case studies will not resolve this problem, because you do not have the status and authority to deal with it. You should refer the matter immediately to a senior member of staff (e.g. your line manager) who will have to take the decisions about how to respond to the parent and what to do. You should inform the parent that you have passed on her serious complaint to senior management. You would also need to take advice about to what extent you can support the pupil because you do not want to interfere in what may become a disciplinary issue.

MANAGING THE PARTNERSHIP WITH PARENTS

Some of the case studies above made the point that it is very important to provide parents with all the information that they need. Case Study 7.8 is taken from one school's information booklet for parents to help them understand what the school provides to support the partnership with parents.

CASE STUDY 7.8

Exemplar and for action/discussion

An extract from Westby High School's Handbook for Parents

We know that children succeed best if they have supportive and informed parents. We value this support, and endeavour to provide opportunities for parents to receive information about curriculum and the general life of the school by:

- our circulars and newsletters;
- parents' consultation and information evenings;
- regular reports on pupil progress;
- making parents welcome parents at any time. We have a welcome room, which is frequently used;
- supporting the activities of the School's Friends' Association, which runs a variety of social, educational and fund-raising events;
- inviting parents to work with us during the school day in the library, office, classrooms, etc.;
- making it easy for parents to visit the school by appointment (or otherwise) to speak to a teacher about anything which is of concern to them.

We expect and encourage all our parents to be partners by:

- providing a welcome room in school, in which parents can talk to teachers;
- offering the facility to make an appointment to meet a teacher during the school day, by telephoning the main school office (e.g. to speak to a teacher on the phone if there are any queries about homework, etc.) – we have telephones in all the main curriculum areas;
- parent/teacher consultation evenings;
- events such as music, dance and drama productions;
- range of Parent's Association activities;
- parents' information evenings related to GCSE, National Curriculum, new developments, etc.;
- keeping parents informed about what is happening in school through our newsletter, bulletin, etc.;
- welcome evening for parents and pupils joining the school;
- wine and cheese evening for Y7 parents early in school year;
- explaining how you can provide support at home for homework and extension study;
- providing the opportunity for parents to do voluntary work for the school, raising money, giving donations or help in kind in school;
- providing a full annual report on each pupil, showing academic progress and other achievements;
- inviting parents to visit school at any time to see children working, view the school and talk to staff;
- providing the opportunity for parents to work for us in school during the day.

The partnership with, and the support of, parents makes the greatest contribution to a child's success.

For action/discussion

- What does your school do to keep parents well informed?
- What kind of information should be provided?
- What do you think is the best way to present it?

MAKING PARENTS FEEL WELCOME

CASE STUDY 7.9

For action/discussion

This is how two schools approach the problem, using vastly different methods.

School 1   Central High School

Several pastoral leaders, with whom I came into contact over the last few years, work in schools which have introduced a welcome room. An experienced year head explains why Central High School established its welcome room.

'Many parents in our catchment area have had a negative experience of education and feel threatened by the school. This makes them reluctant to come into school and we used to have a very poor turnout at parents' meetings and other events. We felt that we had to make a positive statement; so about 4 years ago we set up a welcome room, a small room in which we meet parents. We make every effort to see them even if they turn up without a proper appoint-ment and try to involve them in the life of the school in every way possible. Over the 4 years there has been an effect. Leaving aside the annual meeting for parents, which only attracts a tiny group who want to grumble, on average far more parents turn up to parents' evenings and other functions than in the past. As they began to talk to us more confident, they told us that at the beginning they didn't ask questions because they didn't know whether they should put up their hands when they spoke to a teacher. Now they help us in a lot of different ways and we are really pleased with the way that our relationship with the parents is developing.'

For reflection

How would you organize a welcome room and what should you do to make it welcoming for parents?

School 2   North-Bridge High School: communicating with parents – via the supermarket public-address system

Attendance at school functions and progress meetings was always extremely low, and we wanted to do something about this as a part of our overall drive to improve. We used a staff meeting to brainstorm ideas to bring more parents into school. One of the teachers suggested that we should use the public-address systems at the local supermarkets and community centres to remind parents about the parents' evenings. It felt a bit gimmicky, but we felt that there was nothing to lose and that any improvement would help, so we tried it for the next year meeting in the annual cycle. That was my year group, year 10, and I was keen to try it. It did have an effect. Turnout for that meeting was up on previous year-10 sessions, so we went on using the idea. For performances (school concerts, etc.), we held a poster competition, and displayed the posters all over the shopping parade. We also continued to broadcast announcements about the productions, sports day and other events. We still don't reach the hard core of parents, but the parents' attendance at our events has improved and our relation-ship with the parents is developing.

(The head of year 10 describes an initiative implemented by her school)

For discussion

- Does your school have difficulty in establishing a meaningful dialogue with parents?
- What is attendance like at events and parents' meetings?
- What are the issues raised by the approaches of these two schools?
- Evaluate the solutions and compare them with any initiatives used in your own school.
- What are the lessons to be learned from these schools for you as a pastoral manager?

CASE STUDY 7.10

For action

Communicating with parents – reports

You have received this letter from a parent. Only an extract is given. She is unhappy about the format of the school's reports.

'Reports are most useful to me as a parent when they are clear, honest, constructive and give good advice about how, as a parent, I can help my child. It is frustrating to receive reports indicating that your child has been having problems for some time, but which do not offer suggestions about how parents and teachers can work together to help the child ...'

You are the year head to whom this letter has been sent. You did not design the reports. How do you deal with/reply to this letter?

A checklist for reports

- Are they jargon-free and easy to understand?
- Do they give evidence of achievement?
- Do they indicate areas for further development?
- Do they encourage parental involvement?
- Do they reflect the ethos of the school?

Source: Bastiani (1987, 1988)

BIBLIOGRAPHY AND FURTHER READING

ATL (1999) *Teachers and Parents, a Survey of Teachers' Views*, London: Association of Teachers and Lecturers.

Warwickshire County Council *Reporting to parents training package*, Leamington Spa, UK: EDS Publications.

Alexander, T., Bastiani, J. and Beresford, E. *Home School Policies – A Practical Guide*, Nottingham, UK: Jet Publications.

Macbeth, A. (1989) *Involving Parents*, Heinemann organization in schools series, Oxford: Heinemann.

Bastiani, J. (1987) *Parents and Teachers 1, Perspectives on Home School Relations*, Windsor, UK: NFER-Nelson.

Bastiani, J. (1988) *Parents and Teachers 2, From Policy to Practice*, Windsor, UK: NFER-Nelson.

Chapter 8

Managing pupil behaviour

WHEN A PUPIL'S BEHAVIOUR DETERIORATES OR IS UNSATISFACTORY, WHAT ARE YOUR RESPONSIBILITIES?

As a year or house head, you have overall responsibility for the behaviour of the pupils in your charge. In most schools, though not all, the subject leader is responsible for what happens in the classroom, and you are responsible for everything else. However, if the pupil's behaviour is affecting his/her work in a number of lessons, then the problem is yours to investigate and to try to resolve. Some year leaders or house heads find a conflict between their caring role in dealing with pupil welfare, and their discipline role in managing pupil behaviour and dealing with disruptive pupils. Most of you manage this dual responsibility well, but occasionally this part of your responsibilities is resented by year heads, who feel that too much is unloaded onto them and that they are regarded as the sin bin or dumping ground for disruptive pupils. This happens particularly in schools in which the form tutor has very little pastoral responsibility. Usually the tutor is the first point of reference in dealing with the pupil's behaviour, as generally, when they are concerned about a pupil, in the first instance teachers go to talk to the tutor. In some schools, however, the tutor's role is underdeveloped, the year head has to do rather more than would otherwise be the case, and consequently every minor problem is brought to the year leader.

Defining discipline

Discipline implies 'doing something to someone.' When you manage pupil behaviour you are developing mechanisms which, hopefully, enable the pupils to control their own behaviour better, or at least enable you to influence and manage the pupil's behaviour through the controls you put into place.

Monitoring pupil behaviour

You are often in the position of having to monitor a pupil's behaviour over a period of time to see if there is improvement. In any week you may have several pupils on report. This means that you want to have in place systems which indicate very clearly what the progress over the week has been. In the past, pupils were often issued with blank timetable forms for a week and teachers were asked to comment on behaviour. These forms were rarely specific and the comments tended to be bland or vague. 'OK' was frequently used. Now monitoring is much more precisely targeted.

Two monitoring forms are included below as exemplars. The form in Case Study 8.1 is a general exemplar of how you can monitor a pupil for his/her behaviour. Both forms are two-sided. Note that the form is specific in that it has targets for the pupil to work towards, and that it has been negotiated and agreed between the year leader and the pupil. In this example you write in whatever it is that you want to monitor. Case Study 8.2 takes this approach one step further and is a monitoring form which is designed specifically for dealing with disruption: these exemplars are included for comparison with those you may be using and are easily adaptable.

Setting specific targets

CASE STUDY 8.1

Exemplar 1 A blank behaviour target card

Side 1:

BESTWICK PARK HIGH SCHOOL

Stage 2   BEHAVIOUR TARGET CARD

Name: Form: Date:

Card No.:   Reporting to:

Agreed targets:

1. . . . .

2. . . . .

Signed (pupil) . . . .   Signed (staff) . . . .

Side 2:

Pupil – please give this card to the teacher at the START of every lesson

You must report DAILY to .... To check and sign the card

You must show this card to your parents/guardian to check and sign DAILY

All STAFF – Please check and sign the card at the end of each lesson.

Thank you for your co-operation.

3 = Excellent   2 = Good   1 = Satisfactory   No score = Unsatisfactory

	1	2	3	4	5	6	Total	Staff signs	Parent signs
Monday									
Tuesday									
Wednesday									
Thursday									
Friday									

End of week review: Total for week:

CASE STUDY 8.2

Exemplar 2   School D's monitoring form for disruptive behaviour

If problems occur in your lesson, please tick I or more of the list of possible problems given below or write the problem in the line that is left blank.

Behaviour problems:

- resistance to teacher direction;
- argumentative;
- defiant – disregards teacher's role;
- does not listen to instructions;
- insolent/persistently rude;
- calls out/interrupts;
- talks during teacher exposition;
- talks during pupil activity – too chatty;
- prevents others from working by one or more of the above;
- . . . .

Side 1:

Agreed targets for the week:

I. . . . .

2. . . . .

Signed (pupil) . . . .   Signed (teacher) . . . .

Side 2:

Pupil –   please give this card to the teacher at the START of every lesson
You must report DAILY to your Year Head to check and sign the card
You must show this card to your parents/guardian to check and sign DAILY

All Teachers – please check and sign the card at the end of each lesson.

Thank you for your co-operation.

	1	2	3	4	5	6	Total	Staff signs	Parent signs
Monday									
Tuesday									
Wednesday									
Thursday									
Friday									

Progress made

End of week review:

Teacher's comment:

Pupil's comment:

Dealing with behaviour problems

Beware simply labelling pupils as disruptive. You have to be clear what the problem is. There are two stages to dealing with behaviour problems:

1. observing and recognizing the symptoms;
2. analysing what the problem is really about.

What is going wrong is the first thing that you need to know? Are you dealing with rudeness, lateness, internal truancy, failure to complete work or, as often happens, a combination of factors? This will tell you what the symptoms of the problem are, and indicate what kind of behaviour modification should be applied.

Dealing with the symptoms is only the first step. You really want to understand the causes of the problem to deal with it in any meaningful way.

Pupil behaviour and teacher expectations vary depending on:

- time – according to the day of the week, subject, teacher and other pressures;
- place – in the classroom, corridor, outside the school gates, or at home;

- audience – depending on informal and formal settings (e.g. assembly or mealtimes);
- individual characteristics and labelling – pupils with reputations for disrupting lessons may be treated differently from their peers, or an Afro-Caribbean pupil compared with a white middle-class pupil.

Watkins and Wagner (1987)

Pupil behaviour is also affected by external pressures. Many pupils bring into school problems which adversely affect their ability to concentrate and their behaviour.

How do you improve pupil behaviour?

The behaviour of pupils in a school is influenced by almost every aspect of the way it is run and how it relates to the community that it serves. It is the combination of all these factors which give a school its character and identity. Together they can produce an orderly and successful school.

(DES 1989: 8)

CASE STUDY 8.3

For action

Providing support for a teacher in difficulties

Mireille, a newly qualified teacher (NQT), has come to you almost in tears. Your school is located in a deprived inner-city area and it is not easy for new teachers to establish themselves. Mireille is having major difficulty in establishing her authority on her year-9 classes. This is your year group. She says that she followed procedures by initially discussing the problem with her head of department, but although he has given her some advice about teaching strategies, this is not solving the problem. Listening to her list of teaching strategies being used, the class clearly have no excuse to say that the lessons are boring, but it is obvious that a good professional relationship has not developed between the year-9 groups and the teacher. A geography teacher, she has three groups and she admits that she dreads the lessons. It is currently taking her up to half of the lesson to get the class quiet. She says that it takes her ages to plan lessons that basically she can't deliver. She says that the boys are the main problem. Since she started to play netball after school with some of the girls, they have not been as bad, but the boys are very difficult. There is simply no respect, she says. They do not see why they should co-operate. They argue about everything, claim to have forgotten anything they should have brought, waste as much time as possible and are defiant when she sets detention. Either they are already booked and cannot fit her in, or they make it clear that they will get a note from home to get them off the detention. She feels that she has run out of sanctions and simply does not know what to do next.

For discussion

- What is your role in helping this NQT?
- What can actually be done to improve the situation?

Some steps to helping Mireille

1. Reassure Mireille – admitting a problem is brave and is the first stage of beginning to deal with it.
2. Decide who is the appropriate person to help her – Head of Department (HoD), mentor or you. In this case it is really the HoD or mentor who should deal with the matter (e.g. the mentor should hold some sessions on classroom management as part of his NQT programme).
3. Define what the problem is really about – it appears to lie in her class control and her failure to develop a good relationship with these pupils.
4. Does it have component parts – yes, she is using sanctions more than rewards and they do not appear to be working. Avoiding detentions has become part of the game of taking on the teacher for these pupils.
5. The mentor should take the lead in suggesting possible strategies; these could include:
   - providing some INSET (in-service education and training) on behaviour management – this is an obvious strategy because class control is often the most serious concern for new teachers;
   - rewards tend to work better than sanctions – the mentor should explore this with the group of NQTs;
   - provide some INSET on behaviour management – this is often the most serious concern for new teachers.
6. HoD support could help Mireille:
   - she needs to be seen to have departmental backing in handling these pupils;
   - targeting one or two of the ringleaders. If Mireille can deal with them, the class could well come to order. It has to be done in a way which avoids confrontation and does not enable the pupil to challenge her authority. HoD support is crucial here;
   - reinforcing classroom procedures firmly and persistently pays the best dividends but she may need some support in enforcing them (e.g how the pupils arrive, are seated and depart form lessons); again departmental support could help her.
   - although Mireille has spent a lot of time designing interesting activities for her lessons, the subject co-ordinator should check how well they match the needs and abilities of the year-9 groups. Providing good differentiation still causes teachers difficulty and could be a part of Mireille's problem with these groups.
   - a code for success in geography, keywords attractively displayed and achievable targets could also make a noticeable difference to the learning environment.

7. The year leader's support can help the NQT:
    ● use your year assembly to reinforce standards of behaviour. Three forms in your year group are involved. This is a high proportion of pupils, but they will not all be defiant rebels, most will be followers. You should tell the assembly that it has come to your notice that some pupils in your year group are not behaving satisfactorily in some lessons, that this is totally unacceptable and that you are monitoring the situation on an ongoing basis. This should deter the majority who are not really out to challenge the system, then you will be left with the hard core. These pupils need to learn that they are not going to get away with a poor standard of behaviour, and also that you are aware and will not condone what is occurring;
    ● identifying and isolating the most difficult pupils. Mireille could place a few pupils on report for particular offences, using monitoring forms (e.g. for punctuality, not bringing their equipment or for shouting out or other forms of disruption). Monitoring forms are more useful than strategies, which are only punishments, because here the pupils can be set targets to achieve, which gives you a mixture of supervision and constructive strategies. They also have to be signed by you and given back to you;
    ● when you talk to individual pupils, you could also use your influence with them to make things easier for her. You also need to get the pupils' perception of what has been happening, which may be different from Mireille's view of things. Usually talking to a few responsible pupils can help move a problem forward. Although pupils enjoy a short period of leading the teacher off-task, most prefer to be in an environment in which they can learn, and will know that year 9 is an important year for them;
    ● if detentions have become a major issue, you may need to contact a parent to say that you require the pupil to attend a detention on a particular evening. Involving the parent usually helps, but the parents need to know in what way their child had misbehaved and that s/he is being treated fairly;
    ● if one of the measures is a success form of some sort, it could be productive if it is countersigned by you, so that the pupil knows that his success is known to his year head as well as his class teacher;
    ● invite her to some of the extra-curricular activities for your year group (e.g a football match). It could be useful for Mireille to see her problem pupils behaving responsibly and it would give them something to talk to her about. They would notice and may appreciate that she has come to watch them.

You cannot do it for her, but you can stand visibly behind her.

Low pupil esteem, of course, is an issue that will not simply be confined to one lesson. It is harder to get the match right when you are a beginner, and control is an ongoing problem for new teachers, but it will be a whole-school issue and you should be working with Mireille within the context of the school's approach to successful learning.

Analyse Case Study 3.8 and make a list of the strategies suggested. Compare them with your own practice.

CASE STUDY 8.4

For reflection

Research has shown that a range of in-school factors can influence pupil behaviour (e.g. Rutter *et al.* 1979; Mortimore *et al.* 1988). These factors include:

- environment;
- appropriateness of the curriculum;
- classroom management;
- teacher modelling;
- whole-school management;
- reward and punishment system;
- support systems;
- communications systems;
- home–school relationship.

Source: Blandford (1998)

How many of these factors are relevant to your own school situation?

CASE STUDY 8.5

For reflection

How School F dealt with poor behaviour

In School F, the numbers of pupil fixed-term exclusions had shot up over a 3-year period. To counter this, the school had put in place a tough procedure for dealing with poor behaviour. It was a form of in-school exclusion from lessons, usually for 2 or 3 days. Conditions were stark. The pupils placed on this withdrawal scheme were kept apart from the other pupils at all times. They were put in an outbuilding which resembled stables, with individual stalls. They worked on material set by teachers and the room was supervised at all times by a teacher. It was a form of solitary confinement. During the school's Ofsted inspection, the lay inspector was initially rather worried about this scheme. The headteacher pointed out, however, that the school regarded the scheme as effective because the number of fixed-term exclusions, indeed the number of pupils placed in the school's version of solitary confinement, had gone right down. Most pupils did not go back for a second term. Only a small number of residual offenders now needed in-school exclusion. In conversations with the pupils the same picture emerged. 'We think it is a good scheme,' pupils said. 'You just don't want to go back there, and behaviour in school has improved a lot.' A pupil who had served a second 'sentence' added, 'I tried hard not to have to go back a second time, but couldn't manage it. I am trying really hard now not to be sent there again.' He also said that he thought it was a much better idea than being excluded from school. '*It's not nice, but this way I do some work,*' he said. '*If I'm excluded, I just go fishing.*'

For discussion

- How does this example compare with practice elsewhere?
- What are the lessons of this case study?

What is assertive discipline?

The White Paper *Excellence in Schools* (DfEE 1997) emphasized the need for every school to have a clear discipline or behaviour policy, and stressed the benefits of assertive discipline in schools. I have been asked on a number of occasions, when I have been tutoring pastoral courses, if I would provide a clear definition of what assertive discipline is and how it works.

Basically, it involves the whole school in working together to improve and maintain discipline through a clearly understood behaviour framework, which, although it includes sanctions, emphasizes positive encouragement.

It was first developed in America in the 1970s by Lee and Marlene Canter (Canter and Canter 1976). It was developed because a lot of people believed that school discipline had seriously deteriorated. It was introduced to primary and secondary schools in America in the late 1980s and early 1990s and was revised following these trials. In Britain, however, findings of the Elton committee (DES 1989) did not support the view that discipline was breaking down in British schools. ('*We could provide no definitive answers to the question of whether things are getting worse.*') Assertive discipline was nevertheless adopted by a significant number of schools, and especially by inner-city schools. The programme stresses the need for a positive discipline system that is easily integrated into the teacher's routine procedures for classroom management and is not something extra put in place to deal with misbehaving pupils. It has three essential components:

1. clear unambiguous rules;
2. continuous positive feedback when pupils are successfully keeping the rules;
3. a recognized heirarchy of sanctions, which are consistently applied when the rules are broken.

(DfEE 1997)

It very much builds on the idea of having appropriate procedures in place and keeping to them. The sanctions are graded and recorded. The warnings lead to detentions and letters to parents. Good behaviour is similarly noted and commended or rewarded. Assertive discipline encourages teachers to be consistent in order that pupils come to believe that when they behave in an unacceptable fashion, they will be treated appropriately.

Does it work?

In my experience, it works if it is applied consistently and the rules are totally clear to pupils and understood by them. If they are involved in forming the rules, it works particularly well. It also works best when the number of rewards given outnumber the sanctions. The schools in which this is occurring say: '*We believe in positive discipline and base our behaviour management system on rewards.*' In these schools the quality of the relationships with pupils and the purposeful atmosphere in the classrooms is particularly noticeable. In the schools in which it is least effective, it is not applied consistently. In these schools, the teachers with the weakest class control use the warning system as a threat, which, because the pupils do not respect the teacher, they do not treat seriously. It is also ineffective if the lesson content is not carefully matched to the needs of the pupils. It may be useful to look at Case Study 6.1 on introducing a code of conduct into the school.

Canter and Canter (1992) now suggest that most discipline problems are caused by pupils who do not have positive self-esteem. They suggest three assertive sanctions to use when misbehaviour occurs:

1. in a calm and non-confrontational manner, tell the child to stop the misbehaviour;
2. set out the sanction which will be applied if s/he does not stop;
3. offer the child a choice.

They stress the need for training for staff on how to build a positive relationship with pupils and ways in which to help pupils build up their self-esteem. This includes training in how to:

- guide the pupil towards constructive behaviour by identifying when and why they misbehave;
- develop a whole-school behaviour plan based on pupils' needs;
- handle pupils' anger and attention-seeking behaviour;
- stay calm and assertive when pupils are both disruptive and try to prevent a teacher from teaching;
- succeed with pupils who do not respond to the whole-school discipline policy;
- develop and record action plans.

Key elements of the current assertive discipline programme include:

- establishing a positive relationship with trust on both sides;
- responding to pupils in a proactive manner;
- identifying the needs of difficult pupils;
- developing rules stating the expected behaviour;
- teaching appropriate behaviour through practice, demonstration and praise;
- looking for positive behaviour and praising pupils when they succeed;
- using sanctions which are effective and not vindictive;
- working with parents, senior managers and external agencies as necessary.

CASE STUDY 8.6

For reflection or discussion

From a discussion with some year-9 pupils at School G.

'I'd choose this school again if I had the chance ...' The others nod agreement. Question: Why is that? Answer: The discipline is very good. There's no trouble here. My friends outside school tell me that in their school it is really tough, but here it isn't. The discipline in class is very good, and I like that. There's almost no bullying, and we know that if anything happens the teachers will deal with it at once. I feel safe here ...

Compare this case study with the pupil comments on how School H deals with bullying. What do they have in common? This school has clearly got it right – what are the lessons of this case study?

PREVENTING BULLYING

One of the most high profile of your responsibilities is to prevent bullying. This means that you have to ensure that a programme is in place to make it clear to the pupils in your year or house that bullying is unacceptable. Schools now invariably have a whole-school anti-bullying policy. An exemplar policy is given in Case Study 8.9. You may find it useful to compare it with your own school's policy. If the emphasis is different you may want to think about why this is so.

With vigilance, you should be able to keep the incidence of bullying low, but it is unlikely that any school can prevent it altogether. The pupil's comment in Case Study 8.6 makes it clear that what matters to pupils is that action is taken. Note too that, in the exemplar policy, emphasis is put on ensuring that pupils are not frightened to tell teachers when an incident occurs.

CASE STUDY 8.7

For reflection

School H

'We know that there will be some bullying whatever we do. What I like here is the strenuous effort made by the school to deal with any incident that occurs. What matters to me is that something is done to stop the bully and help the person being bullied. The other thing that I think is really good is that in this school you can take the problem to any teacher. I moved here from another school. In that school there were only one or two teachers to whom you could talk. Here all the staff will listen and help. This really makes a difference ...'

Source: From a discussion with some year-11 pupils at School H.

CASE STUDY 8.8

Exemplar

School C   Anti-bullying policy

Aims and objectives

1. The principal aim is to reduce to a minimum the occurrence of bullying in the school in all its forms, and to create a non-threatening environment for pupils based on mutual respect and concern for the welfare of each other.
2. To create an awareness in the minds of all pupils and parents of:
3. what constitutes bullying;
4. the strategies in place in school which help parents to cope with and resolve any problem associated with bullying.
5. To establish a structure of support for all parties involved in the incidents of bullying (i.e bullies, bullied and parents).
6. To emphasize:
7. the unacceptable nature of bullying;
8. the notion that extreme cases of bullying would expect to be dealt with seriously.
9. To establish confidence in pupils that by sharing the problem with a member of staff, this will not create an even more threatening situation, but will instead lead to a resolution of the problem.

Strategies

These fall into four main categories:

1. raising the profile/recognition;
2. establishing coping strategies;
3. creating a secure environment;
4. dealing with incidents/sanctions.

Raising the profile/recognition

Teaching and welfare staff should be vigilant in their observations of pupil behaviour to recognize and take appropriate action where incidents of bullying occur.

The subject of bullying should be used in assemblies and in subject teaching (e.g Personal, Social and Health Education [PSHE], English, drama and RE) to demonstrate to pupils the school's understanding of what is meant by bullying. This might include:

- name calling;
- excluding one person from a group;
- stopping talking to someone;
- 'hiding' property;

- physical abuse;
- unwanted conduct of a sexual nature, or other conduct based on sex, affecting the dignity of boys and girls at the school;
- unwanted conduct or displayed attitudes based on race, religion or gender.

Establishing coping strategies

- The reluctance of pupils to bring the problem into the open is understandable, nevertheless pupils should be encouraged to report all instances of bullying. This should be reiterated regularly in year assemblies and form time.
- Appropriate action such as walking away, not retaliating and, in particular, finding an adult with whom to share the problem, should be included in any discussions with pupils on the subject of bullying.

Creating a secure environment

- Staff involved in any incidence of bullying should treat all incidents with due concern, which reflects the school's attitude to the problem.
- Pupils should always be sure that concerns will be dealt with swiftly and positively in order to give them security.
- Pupils should be encouraged at all times to find any member of staff with whom they can share their concerns.

Support

- To help the school eliminate bullying.
- Anti-bullying material is used as a teaching resource. An annual audit and short report is produced.
- Strategies are taught to help children deal with bullies. PSHE lessons are used for this purpose and there is at least one special form period per year.
- Our policy is reviewed with staff, governors and students annually in the first half of the school year and is available for parents.
- External agencies and teacher counselling are used to help children.

Dealing with incidents/sanctions

In dealing with incidents of bullying, each party involved should be asked to put into writing his/her own version of any incident. Salient points of any discussions with the pupils should be recorded by the member of staff dealing with the incident. This documentation should be stored in the pupil's file so that any patterns of behaviour, which are forming, will become evident.

Each incident should result in a plan of action being formulated, which should be agreed by all parties.

Any sanctions imposed will depend on the frequency or severity of the incidence of bullying. You will find additional information about sanctions in our *Managing Pupil Behaviour* booklet.

At the appropriate level of seriousness, parents will be invited into the school to contribute to the development of strategies for improvement of behaviour.

Sanctions

To help the school eliminate bullying:

- bullies who physically attack other pupils to hurt them;
- bullies who bring into school and use sharp implements or similar threatening instruments;
- bullies who mentally torment other pupils;
- bullies who make racial or sexual comments;
- bullies who deprive other pupils of their property

must expect:

1. *THEIR PARENTS WILL BE INFORMED;*
2. *TO BE EXCLUDED TEMPORARILY OR PERMANENTLY FROM THE SCHOOL.*

Counselling by teaching staff will be provided and the help of the school doctor, the educational psychologist, the LEA Pupil Services Unit and the educational Welfare Officer will be used depending on circumstances.

Parents are expected to work with the school to ensure that their child is not involved in bullying (including sexual and racial harassment). If they are not prepared to do this, their child will be permanently excluded from the school.

Associated school policies include behaviour, school rules, code of conduct, equal opportunities, pastoral, etc.

'No-blame' approach

The no-blame approach to dealing with bullying was developed by Barbara Maines and George Robinson in the early 1990s (Maines and Robinson 1994), at a time when the problem of bullying in schools was becoming high profile, and because many of the strategies previously adopted in schools were considered ineffective. The no-blame approach is concerned with ending the bullying, rather than punishing the bullies and works as follows.

Step 1   Interview the victim

When a teacher finds out or is informed that bullying is occurring, s/he should talk to the victim about his/her feelings. The emphasis is on finding out who is involved, rather than the specific incidents.

Step 2   Hold a meeting with all the people involved

As well as the bullied and bullies, this session could also include some of those who are on the fringe/periphery of the group of bullies, or some of those who joined in. Groups of six to eight pupils tend to work most effectively.

Step 3   Explain the problem

This is essentially a means of sharing the victim's feelings with the other pupils. Generally drawings, poems or stories are used to convey the victim's distress. The details of particular incidents are never discussed and do not form any part of this procedure.

Step 4   Moving forward

No blame is attributed, but the teacher makes it clear that s/he knows that these pupils are responsible and can change their behaviour towards the victim.

Step 5   Generate strategies with the group

The teachers then asks the pupils for their ideas to move the situation forward and help the victim. Although the teacher responds positively to the ideas put forward, s/he does not insist that they are implemented. No promises are extracted.

Step 6   Leave it up to the pupils

This step involves trusting the pupils to take responsibility for rectifying the situation.

Step 7   Monitor progress

The teacher arranges a date on which to meet the group of pupils to see how the situation has developed.

Step 8   See pupils individually

The teacher holds a short meeting with each pupil involved, including the victim, to see what progress has been made. This helps the teacher check progress and also share feelings which may not emerge in a group session.

The no-blame approach has met with a mixed response. It takes considerable skill and sensitivity to manage it effectively. Realistically, some pastoral leaders will be much better at using it than others, and some educational psychologists and Emotional and Behavioural Difficulties (EBD) teachers believe that the impact of this programme is short-lived. There are also some cases which are so extreme that a no-blame approach simply does not apply. Probably the best thing to do is to develop a range of strategies for dealing with incidents of bullying. Case Study 8.10 is a list of strategies devised by School D to prevent bullying and to deal with it should it arise. It is included as a checklist for you.

CASE STUDY 8.9

For reflection

Bullying: School D's strategies to help you handle bullying

Personal strategies:

- children decide the rights, responsibilities and rules for their class;
- showing respect and dignity in all situations;
- intervention;
- interesting and relevant curriculum;
- whole-class discussions;
- encouraging responsible behaviours;
- communication with lunchtime supervisors;
- no bullying behaviour;
- teaching children about bullying;
- role modelling;
- meeting with colleagues;
- supporting colleagues.

Curriculum strategies:

- case conferences with other staff (consult);
- novels/films/video material;
- school magazine articles/problem page;
- teaching victims coping strategies;
- countering bullying across the curriculum;
- teaching bullies awareness;
- projects;
- discussion/debates;
- PSHE: social skills, negotiation, arbitration, intervention;
- essays;
- English, history, drama, RE.

Institutional strategies:

- contact with primary schools;
- questionnaires;
- inter-agency contacts;
- changing playground environment;
- developing a telling ethos;
- parents' evenings;
- introducing lunchtime activities;
- safe areas;
- bully box;
- training for all staff;
- ongoing staff meetings;
- management responsibilities;
- 'listeners';
- buddy system;
- policy development and implementation

GUIDELINES FOR DEALING WITH FIGHTS AND VIOLENT INCIDENTS

CASE STUDY 8.10

For action

There's a scuffle in the playground. It is only a small group of year-8 boys, but the crowd builds up rapidly and eggs the boys on with whoops and war cries. Some pupils come to the staffroom to tell you because you are the year head – what do you do?

Recent new guidelines from the DfEE (DfEE 1999) have clarified section 550A of the 1996 Education Act, so teachers do now know that they can use 'reasonable force' to prevent anti-social behaviour. This is, of course, the last resort. Your aim is to prevent violence, not to have to separate struggling pupils, but even in the most caring schools incidents occasionally occur and it is important for you to know what you may do and what it is inadvisable to do.

What you may do

Application of force is allowed where teachers may need to:

- physically interpose between pupils;
- block a pupil's path;

- hold – but never round the neck or collar;
- push;
- pull;
- lead a pupil by the hand or arm;
- shepherd a pupil away by placing your hand in the centre of the back;
- in extreme cases (such as self-defence) more restrictive holds.

What you should not do:

- hold round the neck;
- restrict a pupil's ability to breathe;
- slap;
- punch;
- kick;
- twist or force limbs against a joint;
- hold or pull by the hair or ear;
- hold face down on the ground;
- touch a pupil in any way which might be considered indecent.

Perhaps the two most important pieces of advice are:

1. to think before acting;
2. not to take anything personally.

If you start to take the incident personally you are much more likely to lash out and this could lead to trouble. You need to concentrate your thoughts on defusing this situation and taking the heat out of the situation?

Even with the new guidelines, reasonable force is something of a grey area. DfEE circular 10/99 (DfEE 1999) says that circumstances must warrant its use, and that the force used should always be the minimum. The guidance applies in these situations:

- when a pupil attacks a member of staff;
- when a pupil attacks another pupil;
- when a pupil is engaged in, or is on the verge of committing, deliberate damage or acts of vandalism;
- when a pupil is causing, or at risk of causing, injury or damage by accident, by rough play or by misuse of dangerous materials or objects (e.g. in the lab or on the sports field);
- when a pupil at risk absconds from class or tries to leave the school. Remember, however, that you cannot imprison a pupil;
- when a pupil persistently refuses to obey an order to leave the classroom;
- when a pupil is seriously disrupting a lesson.

Dealing with the fight

However much you try to prevent children from fighting, this is not always possible. For example, an incident, such as the scuffle described at the beginning of this section, simply breaks out during break or the lunch hour and, to restore order, you will have to intervene.

The first piece of advice is to take someone else with you. Other staff will be needed to act as witnesses both about the actions of the pupils and the measures used to stop the fight.

It is very likely, especially in boys' fights, that the very sight of a group of teachers advancing on the scene will have an impact. Quite often what looks like an extremely violent fight simply melts away at this point.

It is also common sense to take other staff with you, because one person on their own is unlikely to be able to break up a fight between two or more pupils. If you haul one off, it does not mean that the other will stop. Sometimes, if you intervene on your own and haul one pupil off, the others fly at you. This is less likely to occur if a group of staff deal with the fight. So the advice here is don't put yourself at risk, enlist the help of others.

Another very sensible measure is to remove the audience as quickly as possible. Getting rid of all the non-combatants makes sense because violence thrives on witnesses. It also makes the fight easier to manage.

If possible, use verbal intervention first to give the combatants the time to stop. Reasoning in a calm voice can be effective. As a generalization, it tends to be least effective with a fight between really angry girls.

Assess the situation before diving into the midst of the fight. This could help you end the fight with the minimum of physical intervention.

Think about surprise and noise as more useful than force. A personal warning/alarm or a bucket of cold water could be more useful than another body in the fray.

If you do have to use force, bear in mind the recommendations of what you can do and what you must not do. Protect yourself as much as possible.

If it is really bad, it could be better to call the police.

After the fight is over . . .

Dealing with the pupils

The first thing is to provide a cooling-off period. Normally you keep the pupils apart from each other, and out of lessons until they have calmed down. At this time they can write their 'statements' about what happened, while you inform the senior management team (SMT), if necessary, and their parents.

You will probably need all your listening skills to hear what the quarrel was really about and interpret the perceptions of those involved in order to help the pupils mend their fences with each other.

In the short term, you will impose some form of appropriate sanction on the main combatants. In the longer term, you will be looking for ways to ensure that even a scuffle is a rare occurrence in your year group. Your PSHE programme will need to include a module, appropriately cast for the age and maturity of the pupils, about conflict and non-violent ways of resolving it. It is part of the pupils' development of social skills to learn how to agree and disagree, compromise and back down. If this is a difficult area for you, you may wish to bring in outsiders either to help you plan the module or to deliver part of it. Sometimes it is useful to bring in outsiders the first time, and then you can take over the delivery of the input.

Recording the incident

When you do have to use force it is essential that you record what happened in writing as soon as possible after the incident has occurred. You will need it both as a record of what has happened and for your own protection. It is also important to know precisely what to include in your report.

The incident record should include:

- who was involved – list the names of everyone involved, the time and place and names of witnesses;
- how the incident began and progressed – include details of behaviour;
- what everyone said – make it clear if this is not the actual words used. Try to get it as near as possible;
- what action was taken – describe the steps taken to defuse the situation;
- the degree of force used – explain how it was applied and for how long.

Informing those who need to know

When you have had to use force to defuse a situation, make sure that the SMT or headteacher knows that an incident has occurred. Give them a copy of the report and keep one yourself, just in case you need to refer to what you said.

Remember, whatever you do, to involve the pupils' tutors. They have a right to know what has occurred, and could do much of the work in helping the pupils after the incident. You should also inform the parents of the main combatants as soon as possible after the incident. Immediately you will probably want to use the telephone to put them in the picture, and to give them an opportunity to discuss the incident with you. You may need to book an appointment for this the next day or a few days after the incident, to give time for everyone to get it into perspective. In the case of a very serious incident, or if the pupil has to be suspended, you will, of course, have to inform the parent in writing and ensure that you follow procedures.

If you are really unlucky, the parents will be active participants in the argument between the two pupils, and the quarrel will continue out of school. This kind of scenario is really outside your ability to resolve and all you can do is to try to impress upon the parents the harm that continuing the dispute is doing to their child as well as to others.

Much of the advice in this section is based on materials from the Suzy Lamplugh Trust. As well as dealing with fights when they break out, you want to pre-empt them if at all possible.

CASE STUDY 8.11

For reflection

School L's lunch-hour initiative

School L, a primary school, was concerned about the level of incidents occurring in the playground at break. As part of their move into Investors in People, they decided to offer training to the lunchtime supervisors to help them develop strategies to cope with incidents as they occurred. *'The time spent with the supervisors and the training produced some positive outcomes. Because the supervisors could handle the situations better than in the past fewer real fights developed and pupils were calmer in afternoon sessions. In addition, this training actually helped the lunchtime supervisors develop their understanding of how the school operated. It had an effect on their confidence and self-esteem, and they began to act as full members of the community. We were very pleased with the results of this initiative.'*

Pupil mediation is discussed in Chapter 9 which deals with pupil welfare.

MANAGING A HOME–SCHOOL CONTRACT

CASE STUDY 8.12

Exemplar

The parent promises	*The school promises*	*The pupil promises*
To have high expectations of their son/daughter and to work with the school to ensure that s/he achieves his/her potential	To have high expectations of all students and to work with them to help them achieve their potential.	To work to the best of his/ her ability.
To monitor homework and to encourage their son/ daughter to complete it to the best of his/her ability.	To set and mark homework on a regular basis.	To complete all homework set by the teachers within the deadlines.
To encourage full attendance and punctuality and to notify the school in writing about any genuine absence.	To encourage and celebrate good attendance and punctuality.	To come to school on time, attend regularly and not to truant from or be late for lessons.

The parent promises	*The school promises*	*The pupil promises*
To see that their son/daughter wears the correct school uniform and brings correct equipment and books in a suitable bag.	To set and enforce a clear uniform policy, with regular uniform checks and feedback to parents.	To wear full school uniform at all times, and to carry the correct equipment and books in a suitable bag.
To support the school in reinforcing high standards of behaviour.	To provide a clear code of conduct worked out together with pupils and reviewed regularly, and to insist on high standards of behaviour at all times.	To try to keep the school rules and behave well at all times.
To read the school's newsletter and take note of the dates of meetings and other events.	To keep parents regularly informed of developments in school.	To be responsible for taking home all letters and communications from school.
To attend pupil-progress meetings and other requested meetings.	To make opportunities available for parents to discuss their child's progress with the year head or appropriate member of staff (in addition to the regular progress evenings).	To talk about any problems arising from his/her work with the tutor or year head or the relevant member of staff and with his/her parents.
To work with the school in partnership for the benefit of the child.	To provide an environment which supports the child's academic learning and social development.	To treat students and staff with respect.
	To provide an appropriate, broad and balanced curriculum which caters for individual needs and abilities.	To treat school buildings and property with respect.
	To set and regularly review negotiated targets to help the pupil improve his/her performance.	

This example of a home–school contract is adapted from one developed recently by a LEA for its maintained schools.

What is your role?

The purpose of a home–school contract is to modify a pupil's behaviour and support his/her learning. It is normally invoked when a pupil's behaviour has been deteriorating or has been unsatisfactory for some time. It involves the parent in helping support their child and creates a partnership between the home and the school, which you as the year head have to draft and manage. The exemplar is included to provide a benchmark against which you can check the contract used in your own LEA or to help you draft your own child/school-specific version.

Home–school contracts should present to parents a clear statement of what they can expect from the school and what the school expects from them and their child. It will be clear from the exemplar that the contract should be linked to specific targets set together with the pupil. Action plans or targets 'done to' pupils rarely achieve the desired results. Pupils don't, of course, immediately achieve everything in the plan, but if they are involved in drafting it, you are more likely to achieve some commitment than if it is inflicted upon them. Similarly the time spent explaining to the parents the purpose and the wording of the contract and involving them in the drafting will pay dividends. All of this involves a considerable time commitment on your part. Once the contract is drafted, however, the tutor can manage it on a daily basis, but you will need to monitor the situation and advise or intervene as necessary.

This section links closely to Chapter 7 on your role in managing the partnership with parents.

Managing social inclusion

The 'fine' attached to exclusions means that your headteacher will, if at all possible, want to find means to keep rather than exclude the school's more difficult pupils. This is a change from past practice when there was a growing trend to exclude because of the effect that very difficult pupils had on the school's local image and its recruitment of pupils. The move to deal with these pupils within school rather than exclude them is termed social exclusion and has a clear impact on your workload. You or your deputy head of year, if you have one, or an appropriate colleague will have to act as the progress co-ordinator for the pupil, who needs supervision at all times, including breaks and the lunch hour. Usually, in order to keep them from having an adverse effect on the behaviour of other pupils, they come and go early or late and only attend certain lessons and you will have to resolve the issue of to whom do they report and what facilities are needed. Unless you want to make a rod for your own back, you should create a mechanism whereby they report in to the office (i.e an administrator handles the signing in and out, otherwise this process could interfere with your teaching). The mechanism puts into place an additional layer of monitoring before exclusion and you are likely to be responsible for ensuring that this does happen and that the Individual Education Plan (IEP) is not only in place, but is closely monitored.

An exemplar of an alternative education plan for a pupil under social exclusion is given in Case Study 8.13.

CASE STUDY 8.13

Exemplar

Bestwick Park High School -- Timetable

Name: Darren Smith   Tutor group: IID   Tutor: M. Day   Room: 3

8.30R	Period I	Period 2	Period 3	Lunch	Reg.	Period 4	Period 5
Mon.	Science	Maths	//////			College-link course building	College-link course building
Tues.	Maths	English	Science			//////	//////
Wed.	Work placement at the Sports Centre						
Thurs.	//////	//////	//////			Maths	Science
Fri.	English	IT	Science			//////	//////

Key: ////// = not in school.

Bibliography and further reading and contacts

(1995) *The Anti-bullying Game: A Therapeutic Game for Children*, London: Jessica Kingsley Publishers.

Blandford, S. (1998) *Managing Discipline in Schools*, London: Routledge.

Canter, L. and Canter, M. (1976) *Assertive Discipline in Schools*, Santa Monica, CA: L. and M. Canter and Associates.

Canter, L. and Canter, M. (1992) *Assertive Discipline, Pupil Behaviour Management for Today's Classroom*, Santa Monica, CA: L. and M. Canter and Associates.

Coulby, D. and Harper, T. (1985) *Preventing Classroom Disruption*, London: Croom Helm.

DES (1989).

DfEE (1994) *Pupil Behaviour and Discipline*, Circular 8/94, London: DfEE.

CSIE (Centre for Studies on Inclusion Education) (2000) *Index for Inclusion*, Bristol: CSIE.

DfEE (1997) *Excellence in Schools*, White Paper, London: DfEE.

DfEE (1999) *Social Exclusion: Pupil Support*, Circular 10/99, London: DfEE.

Fontana, D. (1994) *Managing Classroom Behaviour*, Leicester: BPS Books.

Jones, N. (ed) (1989) *School Management and Pupil Behaviour*, Lewes: Falmer Press.

Kidscape *Feeling Happy Feeling Safe*, London: Kidscape.

Suzy Lamplugh Trust: Training Office, London SW14 8AS.

Maines, B. and Robinson, G. (1994) *The No-Blame Approach*, Bristol: Avon Education Department.

Mortimore, P., Sammons, P., Stoll, P., Lewis, D. and Ecob, R. (1988) *School Matter, The Junior Years*, London: Open Books Publishing Ltd.

Olweus, D. (1993) *Bullying at School: What We Know and What We Can Do*, Oxford: Blackwell.

Rutter, M., Maughan, B., Mortimore, P. and Ouston, J. (1979) *Fifteen Thousand Hours, Secondary Schools and Their Effect On Children*, London: Open Books Publishing Ltd.

Smith, P. K. and Sharp, S. (eds) (1994) *Tackling Bullying in Your School*, A practical handbook for teachers, London: Routledge.

Tattum, D. P. and Herbert, G. (1993) *Countering Bullying, Initiatives by Schools and Local Authorities*, Stoke-on-Trent: Trentham Books.

Watkins, C. and Wagner, P. (1987) *School Discipline*, Oxford: Blackwell.

Wilson, J. and Cowell, B. (1990) *Children and Discipline*, London: Cassell Educational.

Chapter 9

Dealing with pupil welfare

As a year head or pastoral leader, one of your main management tasks is to deal with pupil welfare and provide support and guidance for the pupils in your year group or house. This chapter explores the kinds of problem which may arise and discusses how you should carry out this part of your job, which needs tact, sensitivity and the ability to remain objective.

This chapter is concerned with your role in dealing with pupils directly. Chapter 10 will discuss cases concerning pupil welfare in which external agencies become involved.

SOME CASE STUDIES

CASE STUDY 9.1

For reflection

Georgia joined the sixth form to take her A levels. She is a new pupil, who joined the school from a local comprehensive school, which does have a sixth form, but which was not as well regarded academically as our sixth form. You are the head of year 12. When you interview her at the beginning of the year, she is excited to be at your school, and anxious to fit in and do well.

Stage 1

As the year progresses, you notice that socially she is fitting in very well. Some of the most sensible students in her tutor group have taken her under their wing and she is developing a strong group of friends. Academically, you are becoming concerned that Georgia is not really adapting to the demands of the A-level courses. When you read and sign the half-year reports for year 12, the subject comments on Georgia's report do not bode well; she does not seem to be making much progress in any of her A levels.

When you have to talk to a pupil about his/her lack of progress, you normally get a defensive reaction. For example:

- Georgia insists that she has been working as hard as she can;
- the standard, she says, is very different from her previous school. She claims that she now understands what is required for A level;
- she is vehemently opposed to your talking to her mother as she wants to handle the problem herself;
- she promises to work harder.

You definitely need to probe further. Usually it is the case that, in spite of the pupil's denials, there really is a problem and there may be more to it than meets the eye. It is also important that the tutor regularly monitors progress.

Stage 2

You may find that it is just the tip of the iceberg, if so, there will be more developments. For example:

- a few of Georgia's friends come to see you because they think that she is very scared that she cannot make a go of the A levels, and that her family will compare her adversely with her more academic older brother;
- her friends also tell you more about the family situation – mother is an invalid and divorced from father. Georgia has to do a lot of domestic tasks at home;
- one of her teachers comes to tell you he has noticed her working in the local superstore when he shops there in the evenings or on Saturday.

External factors, such as marital breakdown or comparisons with siblings, can affect how a student performs. Often the student has to contribute to the family income or support him/herself through A levels and it is not simply a matter of getting the student to give up their evening/weekend jobs. Generally the student is very reluctant to admit the problem or to let other pupils see that she can't cope. You, or the tutor if s/he has a good relationship with Georgia, will have to talk to the student about her home problems. Talking it through is often useful for the student, who may not be able to see the wood for the trees.

Some strategies you might adopt at this stage:

- set up a programme in which friends, who are studying the same A-level programme as Georgia, go through topics with her and plan questions together with her. This requires a lot from her friends, and the tutor will have to check that the scheme does not peter out;
- ask her teachers to analyse which areas Georgia is finding most difficult;
- provide additional support within the A levels;
- inform the tutor of the family situation and ask her, as part of the monitoring process, to watch Georgia for any signs of stress;
- if possible, involve the parent – but this is less clear-cut for a sixth-former than at Key Stage 3 (KS3) or KS4.

Stage 3

Her work does not significantly improve and by the beginning of summer term Georgia begins to truant – she is spotted on the local station by a teacher going to a meeting during the school day.

As the situation deteriorates, you may have to deal with a very distressed student. Generally the student is trying unsuccessfully to hide her fears about her performance in the subject. When these fears become too much for the student to cope with, or the examination gets nearer, s/he sometimes stops coming to the lessons that s/he finds most difficult or misses whole days. You will have to handle her distress sensitively and firmly and try to sort out her future. The issue now is can you salvage anything for Georgia? You will need all your pastoral skills to handle the situation to produce the best outcome for the student. Possible options include:

- Georgia to give up her A-level course and leave school;
- she starts the lower sixth again – either on a slightly different programme of A levels or a different, more practical course such as GNVQ;
- she transfers to another school to make a new start;
- she returns to her previous school;
- she finds a job at a smaller store, which does not insist on her working two evenings and all day Saturday, because this is too much for her on top of a heavy academic programme.

In the end a package is worked out. Georgia, who very much wants to stay at your school, starts the lower sixth year again, with a slightly different A-level programme. Her subject teachers monitor progress very carefully, setting targets for every stage, which are checked weekly by her tutor. Her mother who, although disappointed and upset about what had occurred, is actually very supportive, and makes arrangements so that Georgia does not have to do as much at home and sorts out the job. Her closest friend, who is now in the upper sixth, offered to continue to mentor her through the lower sixth year and Georgia gratefully accepted this offer. In a very structured environment, progress improved and in the end Georgia did gain her A levels, and a place at the local university.

Note how important it is to unpick all the parts of a problem in order to help and support the pupil.

CASE STUDY 9.2

For reflection

Dissension within the form

You are the head of year 8. Nicola has come to see you because she wants to change her form. She claims that she is unhappy in this form as most of her friends are in the parallel form. You have to tell her that it is not school policy to do this unless there is a very good reason indeed, and that she can easily mix with her friends at break and lunchtime.

You assume that she has accepted this ruling until her mother rings in and asks to speak to you. At the meeting with her mother, a story of cliques and harassment within the form begin to appear. The problem appears to revolve around a boy called Robert, who leads the 'in-group' within the form. Apparently, if you are ostracised by this group, no one will talk to you or have anything to do with you. Nicola has suffered this fate for over half a term. It is affecting her badly and her mother is very worried. For this reason, she supports her daughter's plea to change her form.

When you talk to Robert and his friends, they seem bewildered by the accusations. Robert is a pleasant boy, who has no record of being in trouble with staff, and has a wide group of friends. You notice that most of them, even the boys, are tall for their age and are members of most of the junior school sports teams. They claim that they are not close friends with Nicola, but that there is no real hostility between them. Robert's mother comes to see you, because she is upset that Robert is being labelled a bully. She says that this is totally unfair, and accuses Nicola of being jealous of Robert's popularity. You begin to suspect that the problem does lie mainly in Nicola's mind. Just as you are reaching the conclusion that Nicola wants to join a group who don't want her, and that she has a self-esteem problem, Clare, another pupil in the class comes to see you with the same request as Nicola. She claims that the group controls the form totally and that it is not only girls who are targeted; some of the more academic, less sporty boys are also affected. The problem is real, but very difficult to disentangle.

This is a particularly difficult problem to deal with and you will not be able to solve it speedily. You could spend time trying to make 'the group' admit that they control the form, but you are unlikely to get this admission. Because so much of this problem is subjective and lies in people's perceptions of a situation, you are unlikely to get much real evidence. So what do you do?

A problem-solving approach makes sense in dealing with a problem of this complexity. The problem-solving model can be found in Chapter 6.

1   Diagnose the problem and break it down into its component parts

- A group of pupils, led by Robert, appears to dominate a form and control its actions.
- It does not recognize or accept that this is the case.
- Other pupils are very conscious of the high profile 'group'.
- Deliberately or inadvertently, the group is causing distress to other pupils in the form, whose self-esteem is suffering.

2   Who can help you?

- You should discuss a problem of this complexity with your own line manager, so that any strategies you use have official sanction. It is also very useful to have someone senior to use as a sounding board or to provide advice.

- You may also need outside advice (e.g. from the local counselling or psychological service).
- You should continue to liaise with the parents. Make it clear that you have the interests of all the pupils at heart and that no one will be victimized, and that you will keep them informed of progress.

3 Identify possible strategies

- Clearly you should work in conjunction with the tutor, who must monitor the situation for you and help you apply the strategies. The tutor may need some additional training to help him manage the situation.
- Work will need to be done both to help counsel and support the pupils who are suffering the rejection. Nicola and Clare can tell you how many sufferers there are.
- At the same time you have to work with the group to make their behaviour more acceptable to others. You will have to overcome their hostility to any programme of behaviour modification. You have to make them realize that, whatever their intentions, a problem exists because other people perceive them as 'bullies'. This is a situation in which a no-blame approach is a necessary strategy.
- Robert, the leader, can clearly control and affect the behaviour of others. His influence needs to be for good, rather than simply for his own dominance. The way through to the others is through Robert.
- Opportunities for the group to operate as a group should be limited. The tutor will have to ensure that in-form activities are inclusive and that any groups formed are carefully mixed.
- The Personal, Social and Health Education (PSHE) programme will need to include units which address the issues and which help the form to come to grips with the problem. Including some outside speakers and small-group sessions could be helpful at this stage.

4 Implement the programme of strategies

- Decide the desired outcome and create an action plan to which all sides agree.
- To achieve the result that you want, you will want to apply a number of strategies. Working with those involved separately may however, have to proceed alongside working with them together.

5 Monitor the situation very carefully

- Monitoring will have to be sensitively handled for a number of reasons (e.g. knowing that a careful eye is being kept on the situation will have an effect on how the group behaves).
- The control exercised by the group is very difficult to pin down.

6 Review (e.g. half-termly) and evaluate progress

CASE STUDY 9.3

For action

An unpopular pupil

Jeremy is an able pupil and hitherto very successful academically. His parents are supportive and very ambitious for him. He is under pressure, however, because he is unpopular with other students, especially other able pupils. He has no 'street cred'. Quite often his exercise books and work files mysteriously disappear, and if they appear again, they have been mistreated. Jeremy has to spend a lot of his time rewriting his notes or reconstructing his files. Even though now much of his work is kept on his home computer, anything he brings to school is at risk. Talking to the form, which both you and the tutor have done from time to time when things get particularly bad, has a short-term effect on safeguarding his belongings, but Jeremy regularly suffers taunting and name calling. When it comes to group work, Jeremy is rejected unless the subject teacher insists on his joining a particular group and you have had to instruct the staff to nominate groups in his form. When you talk to the more mature, sensible members of the form, they say that Jeremy is his own worst enemy because he is both arrogant and selfish in his dealings with others. They also say that the majority of the form thinks that Jeremy is sad. Jeremy has started to react by attempting to be a nuisance in class. This is not making him more popular with others, but is affecting his work and progress.

For action

How do you help Jeremy?

CASE STUDY 9.4

Dealing with bereavement

You are the head of year 7. The first day back after half-term you hear that during the half-term break the family of a pupil in your year group was involved in a fatal skiing accident. The mother, the older sister (who was in year 9) and the younger brother of one of the pupils in your year group have been killed, and the girl herself and her father are badly injured. She is now in the local hospital and will be away for some time. Her friends are very upset. They are asking their tutor both about visiting her and about attending the funeral, which will take place at the end of the week. The local primary school, at which the brother was a pupil, has contacted your headteacher because it wants to hold a joint commemorative service with your school.

For action/discussion

The head of year 9 has to help the pupils in his year group come to terms with the death of a pupil in their year. They will need a lot of support. How should this be provided? Your role is more complex. A pupil has lost most of her family. You have to help the tutor provide appropriate support and guidance to the rest of the tutor group is they are to help and support their friend. How do you go about it?

YOUR ROLE AS A COUNSELLOR

Some schools are able to fund a trained specialist counsellor, most, however, cannot afford to do this, and, in your role as a pastoral manager, you have to undertake quite a lot of 'counselling'. In fact, most of what you do is not really counselling; there are different interpretations of counselling and you should be careful how you use the term. Pupils come to you for advice, guidance and support.

If it is to be effective, counselling must be handled carefully and with sensitivity. In this chapter, I shall outline some approaches to counselling, but if you are particularly interested in counselling, you may wish to do a substantial course to give you more of the theory and some opportunities to learn about counselling techniques. A lot of LEAs do run modules on counselling. These are usually a series of twilight sessions spaced over a period of 6 weeks, which include assignments and can count towards qualifications (e.g. for some Open University courses). Some universities also offer this kind of training; so if you want to develop this skill, which can be a valuable asset for a pastoral leader, find out what is available locally and how to get onto the course.

Mainly you counsel pupils, but sometimes counselling is needed for a member of your team, and occasionally you find yourself, usually informally, counselling parents along with their children.

Some steps in counselling

1 Establishing the need

Sometimes pupils come to you seeking help with a particular problem. More often, as in Case Study 9.3, you or one of the teachers notice that something is amiss (e.g. the work of a talented pupil begins to deteriorate). Attendance can also be a symptom, particularly if a pupil is having difficulty on an academic course. Sometimes the form tutor picks up the problem, but asks you do deal with it. Quite often, a few of the friends of the pupil in distress come to see you because they want an adult to be aware of the problem or to seek help for their friend. You have to be sensitive to need; sometimes it is effective to say 'Can I help?' Often, however, initially the pupil will try to conceal the fact that s/he has a problem. One's first instinct is to deny and claim that everything is all right, when clearly it is not.

2 Setting up the interview

Once the need is established, you have to provide the right opportunity to offer counselling. This involves making sure that sufficient time is set aside to enable the problem to be at least aired and to set a timetable for follow-up sessions. In practical terms, you need at least half an hour. Counselling only works in a private, calm, unhurried and undisturbed setting. It is up to you to create those conditions.

3 Encouraging people to talk

Counselling is about getting people to open up and talk about their problems. Initially they are likely to be defensive or find difficulty in talking. Sometimes you will feel that after the first sessions you have not made much progress. This does not mean that you have failed or that you should give up. In fact, you should persevere; but you will need to encourage confidences and draw the person out, using all your sensitive listening skills. There are a number of techniques for helping people to talk:

- *offer reassurance*, so that the person knows that you are not disapproving or critical (e.g. *'Yes, I quite understand why that's getting you down,'* or *'Yes, I do understand'*);
- *be non-threatening*. If you have initiated the session, you may need to take a non-threatening approach (e.g. *'I thought it might be a good idea if we had a chat ...'*);
- *make the setting relaxed*. Sit at a 90-degree angle to the person being counselled, or next to them. Never sit behind a desk when you are in a counselling situation. If a room with easy chairs is available, try to use it;
- *give your undivided attention*. Show that you are giving the pupil your full attention. Do not allow interruptions and maintain eye contact;
- *ask open-ended questions* that make it easier for the pupil to open up to you and describe the problem. It also helps you get a feel of what the pupil thinks the issue is and what really matters to the pupil (e.g. *'How do you feel about that?' 'What bothers you most?'*, *'When do you find that you get most angry?'*);
- *listen carefully*. Demonstrate that you have heard what the pupil has said, by rephrasing and summarizing what has been said (e.g. *'Just let me see if I have understood ...* or *'So you are saying that ...* or *'Have I got it right, you are saying that ...'*);
- *don't say too much yourself*. This is the pupil's opportunity to talk, not yours. Sometimes in order to draw someone else out it can be very useful to share your own experiences, but don't be self-indulgent. Allow a silence to continue and resist the temptation to speak for the person being counselled. Encourage the person to talk by making listening noises such as *'uh-huh'* or *'hum'*.

4 Helping people think through their problems

Having discovered what the problem is, the next step in counselling is to help the person accept responsibility for his/her own problem and to work out his/her own solution. It is his/her problem and in the end, s/he has to solve it. For this reason it is important that you do not offer ready-made solutions. Giving your solution to the problem is unlikely to help, so resist the temptation.

Your aim is to be friendly and encouraging, and, above all, neutral. As well as the listening techniques outlined above, you can use other approaches, such as:

- *sharing* which involves describing, in an open and honest way, a similar experience that has happened to you and how you felt about it. If you use this technique, be concise and avoid taking over the conversation. Beware also of imputing to the person being counselled feelings that are yours rather than his/hers;
- *admit your own fallibility* (e.g. *'I've often made the same mistake ...', 'I must admit, I find that difficult too ...'*).This is another form of sharing;
- *be non-judgemental* – offer relevant advice or suggestions, but do not express your views or criticisms (e.g. *'If you wish, we could allow you to do your homework in the library after school ...', 'You could discuss this with ...'*);
- *ask questions* to solicit ideas and establish alternative ways to solve the problem (e.g. *'So what do you think the options are?', 'How can you avoid getting into that situation?', 'How can you improve the situation?'*);
- *always turn it back* so that it is the person being counselled who controls the agenda, not you. If you have to make a suggestion, phrase it tentatively, or as a question rather than as firm suggestion (e.g. *'I suppose one option could be ...'* or *'Have you considered this line of action?'*).

The main point to remember is to keep asking open-ended questions, as this will help the person being counselled to think through to his/her own solutions.

5   Letting people find their own solutions

The final stage of a counselling session or series of sessions is to try to arrive at a solution to a problem. Remember, the aim is that the person arrives at his/her own solution, even if this is not the one that you personally favour. Once the person has reached this point:

1. accept the chosen solution, even if you have misgivings. Your aim is to help and encourage, so be careful to support any solution, which emerges from the session;
2. agree an action plan and, if possible, a review date. This helps the person to be clear about what s/he is going to do, how s/he is going to do it and by when;
3. make it clear that you would be happy to talk to the person again, not just for the review, but if s/he needs another session to talk, especially if further problems develop;
4. generally the only notes made during a counselling session are agreements (e.g the action plan). Making notes distracts from attentive listening and can be threatening for the person being counselled;
5. do not promise confidentiality. This does not mean that you would normally betray a pupil's confidence, but there are some particularly sensitive areas (such as child abuse) in which you cannot keep a pupil's confidence. Usually, in these

cases, the pupil has come to you because s/he wants someone to know and this will be discussed in the sessions.

6   After the session

You must think carefully about how you handle dealing with the person after the interview. This matters because, for counselling to succeed, you have to suspend any professional authority relationship you have with the person being counselled. It is important to restore the professional relationship immediately (e.g. in the period after counselling), as s/he may test you out and behave in a way which results in you having to apply sanctions.

Your aim after the session/s is to remain supportive in a low-key way. Resist the temptation to check progress too frequently, this puts pressure on the person and is interference. The occasional caring enquiry is fine and is usually appreciated.

Increasingly, attention is being drawn to the number of young people suffering from mental-health disorders. In a recent report, the Mental Health Foundation suggests that as many as one in five young people are suffering from disorders such as anxiety, depression and psychosis (Mental Health Foundation 1999). The increasingly narrowly focused academic definition of raising standards is indicated by recent research showing increased distress in primary school and of new pressures in secondary school.

Case Study 9.5 describes how two schools decided to try to help their pupils.

CASE STUDY 9.5

For action/discussion

Two inner-city schools worked together to help their pupils. Brigtown Hill School is a special school which has a good record in helping pupils with emotional and behavioural difficulties. Brigtown Technology College has a considerable number of pupils, particularly boys, whose behaviour puts them at risk of exclusion. At a pastoral meeting, the year leaders asked if the school could consider some positive methods, which would help the pupils as well as cutting down on the number of exclusions. After some thought and discussion between the senior management team (SMT) and the year leaders, Brigtown Technology College decided to buy into the services provided by the special school, which employed a child and adolescent psychologist for one and a half days a week. The technology college had heard very good reports of the work that the psychologist was doing at the special school, so it bought an additional half day of her time to be used with its own pupils.

It also bought some in-service education and training (INSET) from the special school to help the staff cope better with some of the behavioural problems exhibited by the pupils. To ensure that discipline and treatment did not become confused Brigtown Technology College gave a lot of thought to how the counselling scheme should be introduced, and involved all its pupils in the decision-making process.

One of the most important issues was on which site should the psychologist operate? The head of year 8 explains the problem: 'At first we thought that our pupils would go to the special school to see the counsellor. Brigtown Hill School is situated very near to us, and there would be no travel problem. We thought that it would provide all the advantages of off-site counselling, while belonging to us. We thought it very important to get this initiative off to a good start, so we discussed the opportunity with our pupils, at a special school council meeting. The pupils were keen to take advantage of the opportunity for counselling. They liked the idea, especially as they thought there was less of a stigma attached to a programme operated through the school than having to go to a centre. Even in school, however, they wanted to keep the programme low profile. They did not want other pupils or teachers to know about what they termed their personal lives. A few boys feared that if others knew they were receiving counselling they would be labelled 'loonies'. So there was some disagreement amongst them about where they would like the counsellor to be located. Some of our pupils were very reluctant indeed to go to the special school. A few, however, felt it would label them more to be seen to go to the counsellor here. In the end we took a vote and the majority wanted to have the sessions on our own site; so, although it remains part of the special school programme, we buy the counsellor in to work here one morning a week. Occasionally, when a pupil asks to be counselled off-site we negotiate a special arrangement with Brigtown Hill School. This arrangement provides the flexibility we feel that we need, and some element of choice for our pupils.

The pupils are referred either by their own request, or as a result of their behaviour in school. The year leaders co-ordinate the scheme for the pupils in their own year group, and the pastoral deputy acts as overall co-ordinator and handles the liaison with the special school.

Brigtown Technology College says that, a year on, it is difficult to measure the results. In quantitative terms the scheme is fully used and clearly popular. Exclusions are down this year, and, although the school is reluctant to make a direct link between this and the provision of in-school counselling, it is pleased. The majority of the pupils who go to see the counsellor are those who have resisted having treatment for their mental-health problems for most of their lives. 'Getting them to go was the hurdle we have jumped over. Once they get to know the counsellor, they no longer mistrust her, whereas a clinic was too daunting an experience for them. Looking back on it now, we should have realized much sooner that a considerable number of our pupils had unresolved mental-health problems, which affected their behaviour and progress. These problems needed to be tackled,' the head of year 11 voices the thoughts of the pastoral team. She is now monitoring whether there is any effect on attendance in the last and vital year of compulsory education. At the most recent year-heads' meeting, they were discussing whether they could afford to buy an additional half day of the counsellor's time.

The scheme has also led to some other collaborative initiatives with the special school and the pooling of expertise, and some flexible use of facilities is viewed as advantageous for both sides.

For discussion

- What are the lessons of this case study for you as a pastoral leader?
- How frequently are the pupils in your school screened for mental-health problems?

INVOLVING OTHER PUPILS – PEER-SUPPORT SCHEMES

Peer-support schemes are regarded as helpful means of fostering pupils' emotional development and their social skills. Case Study 9.6 describes how one school developed an inexpensive extra-curricular activity to help the social development of its year-7 pupils.

CASE STUDY 9.6

For action/discussion

Downly High School is an inner-city secondary school with a large number of pupils with behavioural difficulties. It particularly wanted to help the pupils develop their social skills in an unthreatening environment. One member of the pastoral team had previously worked in a primary school. She suggested that what was wanted was a regular extra-curricular session for year-7 pupils which involved fun activities and also some circle time, which would help them develop their social skills. She suggested that year-12 and year-13 pupils could act as leaders for these sessions.

The pastoral team found this idea attractive. It was simple, inexpensive and had a lot of advantages. They might need to buy in some expertise initially, but over time there could be a lot of benefits for the school and its pupils.

The pastoral team gave a lot of thought to how the plan should be implemented. It was very important that it worked successfully, and that it was an enjoyable experience for leaders as well as the year-7 pupils. It would also give the year-12 and year-13 pupils a valuable learning experience and status and 'empower' them. They decided that the first year would be a pilot, a learning experience for them, and that they would review and adapt the scheme after the first year.

There was a lot of discussion about how the pupils should be selected for the scheme. The year leaders' desire to make it a voluntary activity conflicted with the need to target particular pupils. The head of year 7 suggested that they use the information they received from the primary schools to identify a target group and that the opportunity should be offered to all the pupils so identified. During the year, the data built up on the pupils and work with the external agencies could lead to more pupils being added to the list. The head of year 9 suggested that the local psychological service should also be consulted and offered the opportunity to participate in the programme, with representation on the planning group. There was some laughter at this suggestion, because it was always difficult to set up a meeting with the schools' psychological service. Nevertheless, it was felt to be a good idea to inform the service of the school's initiative and ask for advice/suggestions and guidance. This was done. In fact the psychological service liked the scheme very much. They sent a representative to the next planning meeting and were particularly helpful in providing guidance about which pupils would benefit most from being offered the opportunity. At their suggestion the planning group also liaised with social services. They also made some helpful suggestions about how the scheme could be monitored.

The guidance from the psychological service and the prior experience of the year-8 leader led the team to structure a scheme that offered a different group the opportunity each term. Ten or twelve pupils at the most could be targeted at one time and would form a club. Next year, if the scheme worked well, two groups could run at the same time. It was felt that it was wiser to run one group well this year rather than to do too much before the expertise had developed.

The leaders could work in pairs or threes so that they did not have to take too much responsibility and were part of a team. It was felt that year-12 and year-13 pupils would need definite training to carry out the task, but that this activity could form part of the practical work that they did for their childcare GNVQ course and lead to certification. Both sides could benefit from the arrangement.

There was a lot of discussion about the need to have an adult on the premises. It was pointed out that for the first hour or so after school, which was when the club would operate, there was invariably someone working in the staffroom and that legally this would be adequate. The year leaders felt, however, that for the first year they wanted to provide more back-up for the sixth-formers and they volunteered to work on a rota basis in the staffroom at the time the club was operating. This would give the year-12 and year-13 leaders security without any overt staff interference.

Facilities were not a problem. One of the large year rooms could be made available on a regular basis and the field or a large hall could be booked occasionally.

The pupils would be given the opportunity to name the clubs and some choice about the activities included in the programme. This would contribute to the pupils' ownership of the initiative. Tea (i.e. squash, biscuits and crisps) would be provided to ensure that the pupils were not hungry and to make the activity a pleasant experience. An outing would also be included in the 10-week programme, and the school would have to budget for this and make arrangements for any transport.

Arrangements would have to be made to ensure that there were no problems about the pupils' journey home. Downly High is an inner-city school, so most pupils use public transport or walk; but the letter to parents included a question about how the pupils would get home after the course and individual arrangements were made.

Parental consent was essential before a pupil could be included in the programme, so letters were sent to all the parents and a session for parents to explain the scheme was arranged before the initiative started. Attendance at parents' meetings was always an issue for the school, and for this reason much thought was given to how to entice the parents into school to attend the meeting. Year-7 parents were, however, more enthused than other year groups, and for the pilot we did not need a huge take-up. If the scheme proved popular and successful, getting the parents to attend next time would be easier. The school could also use some pictures of the clubs in operation as promotional leaflets for next time. The meeting was made into a social event, including coffee and an opportunity to meet the form tutors and to hear about the scheme. Quite a lot of parents attended and showed interest, especially when they realized that they would not have to pay anything. A few phoned in to say that, although they could not attend for various reasons, they were interested in this opportunity for their son/daughter and could they be kept informed. As long as the parent had made contact and signed the consent form, the pupil could participate.

Acting as club leaders proved a popular activity for our year-12 and year-13 pupils. There was no shortage of volunteers. It became competitive and leaders were chosen both for what they could contribute and what they could gain, and teams were made up with a mixture of strengths. A good link formed with the local university and a teacher-training course helped the school to provide training for our volunteer leaders and monitoring was built in for the leaders to provide the assessment needed to help them earn credits. The college also helped us to devise the written tasks and assignments, which the group leaders would have to complete to earn their credits.

It had to be explained to year-7 pupils that the occasional adult would come to monitor the group leaders. For year-7 pupils, this was the least popular element, as it was felt to be intrusive. Downly High School is still working on how to reconcile this need for the sixth-formers with the need of year-7 pupils to bond only with the leaders.

The college and psychological services helped Downly High to develop a range of activities for the clubs, but over time others have been introduced, and existing activities are developed and refined to meet needs. Circle time is always a feature of the session. At first, there was some scorn, as pupils remembered this as a primary-school activity, but rapidly it become a central part of the routine. It encouraged pupils to speak in a non-threatening environment, to listen to others and to share experiences. The leaders' training helps them to cope when emotionally demanding experiences are shared. Sometimes this can lead on to the pupils seeing the counselling service; more often, once they have shared with other pupils, pupils are able to talk to their year leaders about their problems.

There was some concern initially that a 10-week scheme was insufficient and that the social skills developed during this time would be lost when the pupil left the group. In fact, the school has found that, unlike some of the intensive reading schemes which have to be sustained if the pupil is to retain the skill, social skills are retained.

The pupils enjoyed the club and wanted it to continue. They grieved for the club and had to have help to deal with their grief. The year leader had to explain very clearly that other pupils also had to be given a similar opportunity. They offered a reunion social at the end of the year for all pupils who had taken part in the clubs, and this gave the pupils something to look forward to.

The scheme has now operated for 2 years. In the second year, two parallel groups ran each term, involving some seventy-two pupils. The staff noticed fewer fights in year 7 and staff reported better interaction in class discussion and generally more positive relationships than in some previous year groups. This standard was maintained when the pupils entered year 8, and, although it is difficult to evaluate precisely, the school feels that the pupils have learnt better coping skills as well as generally improving their social skills. At the end of the second year of the scheme, the school intends to ask the college to carry out an evaluation for them and to modify the scheme in the light of the findings.

Downly High School is now looking at how they can extend the scheme to enable the whole of year 7 to participate. It is also building into its year-7 PSHE programme a session in which the pupils are clearly told about the extra-curricular sports and other opportunities available to them as year-8 pupils. Year-8 pupils are the speakers in this session.

For discussion

1. Compare this successful introduction of change with that described in Chapter 6 'Introducing change'. What features do they have in common? Schemes in which year-12 and year-13 pupils help younger pupils with their reading have also worked well in a number of schools.

2. How can the experiences of these schools be adapted to help the pupils in your own school?

PEER COUNSELLING/MEDIATION

CASE STUDY 9.7

For reflection

A year leader from Moulton Middle School describes how her school introduced a peer-mediation initiative

The suggestion to introduce peer counselling came through school council. At a meeting which discussed the increasing problem of conflicts between pupils and the aggression which had been increasing recently, especially at lunchtime, pupils said that they wanted to provide a positive system in which pupils helped each other. As year heads, who sometimes despair of getting pupils to take responsibility for their own actions, we were very pleased and wanted to take on board the idea, but we weren't sure what it entailed. How should the pupils be selected, what would they have to do, how much responsibility would they have to take and what training would they need? These were just some of the issues raised at our meeting. We were also unclear about how we would monitor the system.

Because we had so little information it took us a while to get started. The first group we approached was our colleagues in neighbouring schools. We raised the issue at the area pastoral meeting. Nobody locally was doing it though there was some interest. Colleagues believed that some London schools were operating this kind of approach, though they could not name any, and someone had heard about a scheme in Bristol, so we tried to find out more about it. Bristol was too far away for us to become directly involved in the scheme, but we could use it to spark off ideas and perhaps to benchmark against, so we contacted the Education Department in Bristol. Time passed and we thought we would not get a response, then the Bristol Mediation Schools Project sent us some information, which we found helpful. For a start they provided us with a definition of mediation: 'A process of peer mediation in which those in conflict are guided by an equal through a series of steps so that they can find their own solution to the problem.' This was what we wanted to introduce, now we needed to work out how to do it.

We also consulted a local counselling service and they stressed the importance of good training and support for the pupil mentors and offered to run an awareness-raising session for staff and a programme of training sessions for our pupils. The sessions would concentrate on helping the pupils develop their communication skills. They would explore conflict and co-operation, learn effective listening skills and how to express their feelings and echo and restate the feelings of others. The training would help the pupils to develop skills in seeking out and reinterpreting different points of view and in not taking sides.

We wanted to take advantage of this offer, as this kind of training would help our pupils generally in developing friendships and good relationships with others as well as raising their self-esteem, but the PSHE budget was too small for us simply to book the training. Besides, we needed SMT support before we adopted this approach; so, as a group, we went to see the headteacher. The head was extremely interested in the idea. She had been very concerned at the increase in aggressive behaviour and finds it very difficult to get lunchtime staff at all, let alone quality lunch-hour supervisors. She promised to try and find us the necessary funding, though she feared that it might have to wait for next year's budget. After some discussion with the bursar, however, the school managed to find the money to pay for the training programme.

Now we had to decide how to select the pupils. We decided we wanted to involve the pupils in as many of the decisions as possible, so we consulted year councils. Pupils were more sensible and responsible than we had expected. They appreciated that to get value for money we would have to train as many pupils as possible in the first round. They pointed out, however, that, although there were benefits to being trained by outsiders, a member of staff could be trained to run further programmes, and each one of the year councils in turn decided that this would be acceptable to them.

Feedback from pupils' discussion made it quite clear that they wanted the trainees to be volunteers, not pupils regarded as suitable by the staff. The counselling service also advised us that pupils, who had been bullies or exhibited aggressive behaviour, would benefit from the training, and even if initially no one selected them as a counsellor, their interactions in the playground were likely to improve. Following these discussions we announced in year assemblies that those interested in the training should give their names to the year head. This strategy would show us the level of interest. If interest was low we could train all those who offered, if too many volunteered, we should have to use some kind of selection process. In the end the scheme attracted quite a lot of pupils, spread quite widely throughout the school, but not so many that we could not train them as one group. A few of our most difficult or volatile pupils volunteered, and, although we had some concerns, we followed the advice to train everyone who had offered their services. The training took place over a 6-week period and all the pupils who had volunteered completed the course.

It was becoming clear that we were moving towards introducing two allied initiatives – a playground-mediation scheme and a peer-counselling scheme. Pupils could be involved in either or both. The two initiatives would help us in managing both pupil behaviour and their welfare.

Now we were ready to start the schemes operating. The playground-mediation scheme is fairly easy to operate. The pupils work in pairs in the lunch hour to help other pupils solve their disputes. Initially we paired the stronger pupils with the less confident, but after the first year we let the experienced volunteers choose their partners, but always provided an experienced partner for new volunteers. At first, there were some problems with lunchtime supervisors who did not understand the scheme or recognize the position of the mediators, so we provided some training for lunchtime supervisors to increase their understanding and to help them support the mediators. One of the year-head team meets with the mediators on a regular basis in order to pick up any problems.

Mediation works if both pupils want to resolve their differences and are willing to go to the mediator. Where a conflict has developed, the pupils are invited by the mediators to withdraw to a more private place, where there is no 'audience' to wind up the participants, and to discuss the situation with the mediators in confidence. They explore together facts, feelings and possible options to help the disputant come up with strategies to move the situation forward. They are trained not to offer advice, but to be non-judgemental and to support the disputants towards creating their own solution to the problem. They do, however, keep a brief record of what has occurred. The mediators do not deal with fights, should they break out, but it is clear to both pupils and staff that far fewer disputes develop into fights than in the past. Staff also remarked on the improved self-confidence in pupil conduct. The main gain for the school is an improvement in the school atmosphere as the mediation stages create a safe and disciplined atmosphere in which conflicts could be and were resolved.

We had to provide some private space for the counselling scheme. This was difficult for us, but eventually, after some creative thinking, we identified a small area which would not expose pupils too obviously to their peers if they visited it. It needed decoration and, after some negotiation with the support staff and site manager, we were allowed to offer the pupils the opportunity to paint and furnish the room. We were deluged with volunteers for this activity, so we decided to keep it within one year group, balloted it and year 6 succeeded and much enjoyed themselves.

Our peer-counselling scheme involved pairing older, usually year-7 pupils, and younger pupils together to help the younger pupils gain experience of problems. It has proved very valuable in developing self-esteem and willingness to take responsibility among the pupils serving as counsellors, especially our year-7 pupils, our top year group; but there have been gains at both ends. The younger pupils say that one of the things they like about the scheme is that the year-7 pupils have been able to relate their own experiences to the needs of their partners, and they like to talk problems through with someone not much older than them.

The two allied schemes are now firmly established and valued components of what we offer our pupils.

A scheme in which sixth-formers provide support for younger pupils is described in Chapter 11.

BIBLIOGRAPHY AND FURTHER READING

Mental Health Foundation (1999) *Bright Futures Report'*, London: Mental Health Foundation.
UK Government (1994) *The Report of the Hunt Committee*, London: HMSO.
Gilmore, J. and Diamond, P. (1993) *The Listening School* (two vols), Pontesbury: Links Educational Publications.

Chapter 10

Liaising with external agencies

Your responsibility for pupil welfare involves you in a considerable amount of liaison with external agencies. For example, you have to negotiate and liaise with social workers (who operate the Children's Act from within a social-services department), education welfare officers (EWO, who respond to absence) and educational psychologists (who make assessments of special educational needs). This chapter explores this aspect of your role and provides detailed case studies against which you can benchmark your own practice or that of your school.

MAKING EFFECTIVE USE OF THE EWO

One of your responsibilities is to monitor pupil attendance. Research has indicated that absence has more effect on a pupil's progress than any other single factor. In some areas the culture of attendance, especially in Key Stage 4, is not well developed. Pupil absence steadily increases in the last 2 years of compulsory education and, all too frequently, the parents condone the absences. It is very difficult indeed to do much about attendance in year 11, but generally, if problems develop, your main external support is the EWO. The title varies but basically the work of an EWO concerns pupil attendance. The role of the EWO is no longer negotiable between schools and the LEA. It is governed by service agreements, drawn up in advance with clear targets and time allocations. In some areas, however, it is very difficult to fill these posts which are not well paid; so, sometimes a long time goes by in which there is no EWO available. In most cases, however, an EWO is attached to the school and visits regularly, sometimes weekly, to check absences and agree follow-up in cases which cause concern. If cases are followed up in the early stages, it is sometimes possible to prevent them from developing into residual truancy. Using the EWO thus extends and supports your own work with the family.

SOME EXAMPLES OF CASES WHERE INTERVENTION BY THE EWO COULD HELP

CASE STUDY 10.1

1. Terry was never a highly motivated pupil. Now he is in year 10 and his attendance is clearly slipping. There have been a series of absences, usually a day at a time, and the notes are not keeping pace with the absences. You suspect that Terry is beginning to truant. You have phoned home, but either no one is in or your inquiries are met with evasions. In this type of situation, the EWO is your best means of following up the absence and improving Terry's attendance.

2. Anne-Marie's mother is an invalid, and Anne-Marie has always had to help a lot at home. Occasionally this has affected her attendance, but the school has understood about the situation. Now, however, the marriage has recently broken up and her mother has become too dependent upon Anne-Marie. The absences are always covered by a note, but are becoming much too frequent and are beginning to affect Anne-Marie's progress. Her mother is preoccupied with her own problems and does not seem to understand. It is not school policy for year heads to undertake home visits, so it is clearly time to bring in the EWO to visit the family.

DEALING WITH SOCIAL SERVICES

CASE STUDY 10.2

For action/discussion:

Attending a case conference

You are the head of year 9 in a school not far from London. During period 1 you receive a phone call from social services. Jessica was picked up by the police in central London last night. Jessica would not co-operate with the police and had spent the night in a cell. Now that her identity had been established, social services have been contacted and, in turn, they are informing you that Jessica will be absent today as she is still in the hands of the police.

Jessica already has a social worker dealing with her problems, because she is not getting on well with her parents, especially her stepfather. Last night she was with a much older boy. When the police searched him, they found drugs on him. Social services want to hold a case conference urgently to make some decisions about Jessica's immediate future. They tell you that Jessica will be with them by this afternoon and they would like to hold a case conference. Both parents will be attending and they would like you to attend.

What is your position and responsibility in this matter?

Normally the school would want to have a representative present and, as the year head, you are the person who is likely to be best informed about the pupil. In this case, because the police have been involved, it is almost certain that the school will make it possible for you to attend. If the timing of the meeting makes it too difficult to release you from your lessons, then usually a member of the senior management team (SMT) attends. Providing full briefing for someone else, and later on getting the feedback from the meeting, is always more difficult than attending yourself – go yourself whenever possible.

BEFORE YOU ATTEND

It is very important to be fully prepared for the case conference

Inform the tutor

You should inform the tutor where his absent pupil is and that a case conference is to be held. If you can only give partial information, make it clear that currently you cannot tell the tutor everything, but you will keep him informed as the case progresses. You also want to consult the tutor, because he may well know the pupil better than you do, and he should be able to contribute to the picture that is building up.

Make sure that your information about the pupil is up to date and comprehensive

In order to decide where to place the girl, Social services may well want information about her progress and behaviour in school. This means that you have to check the information you have on file about Jessica. There are three main areas.

1   Check the pupil's attendance over the last half-term

You want to see if there is a pattern and if Jessica's recent absences have been covered by a note. It may transpire that she has been out and about with the boyfriend during school time as well as at night and you want to be sure of your facts here. In this case you learn from the tutor, Mr Turner, that there have been occasional day's absences recently. A note always covers these absences, but the notes are rather vague and Mr Turner is not perfectly sure about the signature. He had been meaning to talk to you about this, but, as all too often is the case, had been overtaken by events.

2   Check up on the pupil's recent progress at school

You may have to arrange a 'round robin' personally to get this information on time, and will want to compare the current situation with her last report, and possibly take a copy of this with you. In this case, it is clear that Jessica is an able, but not very motivated pupil. Her work is consistently satisfactory and usually submitted on time. There are no academic problems, and she could do well at GCSE, but her teachers think she is coasting and that she is not responsive to opportunities provided to do more than necessary.

3 Check whether there have been any incidents concerning the pupil's behaviour

One of the things that you want to know is whether there has been any recent deterioration. In this case, although occasionally she can be argumentative, Jessica does not usually give any trouble in class. She has not been reported to you by anyone recently. Her tutor and other staff consulted have not noticed any change, but they say that she is normally a rather reserved pupil, with occasional strong opinions expressed mainly in Personal, Social and Health Education (PSHE) or English discussions.

Liase with your line manager or a member of the SMT

You will need to inform your line manager of the situation and get permission to attend the case conference. It is important that someone attends and, if you can't go, the pastoral deputy may have to represent the school. You also need to discuss the problem and clarify the school's view of the situation. What do you consider would be best for the pupil? In this case, the main in-school issue appears to be attendance, which you will certainly need to monitor. The SMT, however, voices some concerns about the drugs, and you will need more information here. Nevertheless, it seems you are likely to be looking for a solution whereby your pupil can continue to be educated at your school. At the meeting one of your responsibilities will be to put forward the school's view.

AT THE MEETING – WHAT IS YOUR ROLE?

First, you are representing the school at a conference which will make some immediate decisions about the pupil.

One of your roles is to listen. You are present to learn how the different parties view the situation. In this case, the animosity between Jessica and her stepfather quickly emerges. He has been married to her mother for 3 years now and Jessica clearly resents him and does not accept that he has any right to participate in decisions regarding her future.

It also becomes clear that, although quiet and well behaved at school, at home Jessica is very strong willed. Since she met the boyfriend, William, she goes out at night regardless of her mother's instructions not to do so. William appears to be an area of major disagreement. He is several years older than Jessica and has a police record. Jessica's parents don't like this relationship at all and a row breaks out between Jessica and her parents during the conference. She does not want to go home with them and is very disrespectful, using language that she certainly does not use at school.

You are there to provide information about the pupil's progress, behaviour and attendance at school, so that the social workers can build up an overall picture of what is happening. In this case, the school appears to be an oasis of peace in a fairly turbulent life, and you will want any decision taken to enable her to continue to attend the school. You offer to liaise with the school EWO about attendance.

Jessica is sent outside while the adults present discuss the case. This worries you as you suspect that, if no one keeps an eye on her, she may 'bunk off'. When you voice your concern, the social workers reassure you, explaining that there is a clerical worker in the outer office, so you persuade them to phone through to the secretary to get her to tell the social workers immediately if Jessica shows signs of leaving the building.

Now that Jessica has been sent outside, Jessica's parents are encouraged to share their feelings about the situation. They are both angry and distressed. They want their daughter to come home with them, but social services are concerned that if she goes with her parents, she may simply run off. They suggest a cooling-off period of a week or so in local-authority accommodation with a family, while they mediate between the girl and her parents and work to repair the relationship. Jessica's mother becomes very tearful at this point. She regards the idea as shameful and as indicating that she has failed as a mother, and the social workers have to work hard to persuade her that a cooling-off period could have some positive advantages.

You are entitled to raise points which concern you. For example, you are suspicious that Jessica has been missing school sessions to meet William and raise the issue that Jessica may want to be away from her parents because she thinks it could be easier to meet William than if she were at home. The parents support this point, they are very anxious about the influence that William may have on Jessica. The social workers tell you, however, that when they informed William that Jessica is only 14, he appeared very surprised and claimed that she had said she was 17. This is credible, as Jessica can look quite mature in her out-of-school clothes. The senior social worker indicates that, although he can't be sure about this, he thinks William will dump Jessica now that he knows she is only 14. During this discussion you raise the issue of the absence notes and discover that, although most of them have genuine signatures, Jessica has been pressurizing her mother into signing notes, when actually she has not been sick. You also notice a bruise on Jessica's mother's arm, and ask a pertinent question about whether Jessica's tactics include physical force. When he realizes what has been going on at home, the step-father becomes very angry and accuses Jessica's mother of being much too soft with the girl and giving into her on every count. He now wants something done urgently about Jessica.

You also think that Jessica may need some counselling to help her build a better relationship with both her parents, and particularly her stepfather. She clearly had a very close relationship with her mother before the second marriage. Indeed, a significant part of the problem could be Jessica's resentment of being supplanted in her mother's affections by a stepfather. It could also be affecting her choice of boyfriend. Your school is fortunate in having a part-time counsellor. You would like Jessica to have some sessions with the school's counsellor, but both the parents and Jessica would have to agree to this. As an alternative, you suggest the local Way-In Counselling Service, which would provide counselling in a non-school situation. This option could be better as Jessica's problems do not centre on school.

You also want information about the drugs which the police found on William. You need to know if this means that Jessica is taking drugs. If so it could affect the school's willingness to take Jessica back. The social worker says that only soft drugs are involved, and that there is no evidence that Jessica has been using them. Social services would like the school to give Jessica the benefit of the doubt.

At this point the stepfather intervenes. He maintains that the present situation is unbearable, and cannot continue. He is also of the view that, if her mother cannot control Jessica, she should be sent to boarding school. This suggestion reduces Jessica's mother to tears once again, but it has an effect and, in the end, Jessica's mother is persuaded to agree both to Jessica going to local-authority accommodation for the time being and to the whole family receiving counselling.

At this stage Jessica is retrieved from the outer office. She is clearly relieved not to be going home with her parents. This has the effect of making Jessica's mother break down again, and the stepfather has to comfort her. Jessica is not keen to have counselling. She is even less keen on the suggestion, interjected into the discussion at this strategic point by her exasperated stepfather, that she should go to boarding school. She also definitely wants to stay at her present school. Although you suspect that this has more to do with accessing William and avoiding the strict rules of a boarding establishment than love of your school, you do want to keep her as a pupil. She agrees to see the school counsellor in the first instance, and the social workers ask you to make the arrangement. When the social workers have made the necessary arrangements for Jessica's temporary accommodation, the conference ends and her parents leave.

Before you leave, you stress that you need to be kept fully informed of developments in regard to Jessica's case and the social workers agree to do this.

AFTER THE MEETING

You will want to make clear, concise notes on what has been discussed and decided at this meeting and you should place this information on Jessica's file.

You have to provide information about the case conference to a number of people:

- for a start, you must report back to your senior managers the main points of the conference and what decisions were made in regard to the pupil;
- you should also brief the tutor (e.g. Jessica's attendance has emerged as an issue and will need to be monitored carefully);
- arrangements will need to be put in place for Jessica to see the school counsellor;
- although Jessica has probably selected this as the softest option available, counselling could help her. Once counselling has started, it is between the pupil and the counsellor, and you should not interfere;

- because attendance emerged as an issue, you must also contact the school's EWO and put her in the picture. Once you have done this, the EWO should keep an eye on the situation.

For discussion

- What are the issues involved in this case study?
- What is the role of the school and, in particular, of the year head in a matter than is not really about the pupil's progress in school?
- Most schools do not have their own counsellor -- where can you send a pupil?

YOUR ROLE IN LIAISING WITH THE CHILD PROTECTION AGENCY

CASE STUDY 10.3

For action

Derrick, a year-8 pupil, is found late one night wondering the streets in obvious distress. When questioned at the local police station, he said that he was afraid to go home, because his mother worked shifts and her boyfriend, who lives with them, keeps 'hurting' him. On examination, there are signs of attempted buggery and other bruising and some tears to his anus, which gave the appearance of having occurred over time. To help the Child Protection Agency make an assessment of the case, the Social Services Department convene a case conference and ask the school for a report on Derrick's recent behaviour and progress at school. The deputy head, who is the school's named person for child protection, asks you to collect the information for the report and to talk through the case with her.

Derrick is a quiet boy with no behaviour problems and little on his file. You do not know him well. His most recent report indicates that staff feel that Derrick could do better. Their comments indicate that the pupil appears to lack motivation and has a rather short concentration span. Your 'round robin' to staff asking for up-to-date information about his progress reveals that homework is not being completed and that Derrick has not been very responsive to the teachers' efforts to get him to work harder and improve his performance.

You have a word with Derrick's tutor, both to put him in the picture and to fill out the picture, and become very concerned at what you learn. The tutor tells you that Derrick, who is always a rather reserved and solitary pupil with few friends, has been particularly withdrawn recently, except in one PSHE discussion on family relationships, in which he was vehemently anti-family and then almost weepy. After the lesson, the tutor didn't follow this up, as Derrick never wants to talk to teachers.

The tutor added that, now that he comes to think of it, recently Derrick has taken to hanging around the form room after school, and he has had to ask the boy to leave. The tutor hadn't thought anything of it, and he hadn't thought to tell you. *'How was I supposed to know?'* he demands, indignantly. *'We need INSET [in-service education and training] on what the signs of child abuse are and how to spot them. I didn't know what to look for!'*

For discussion

- What went wrong and why?
- What policy issues do this case study raise?
- The tutor's attitude clearly indicates that he feels it is your fault for not briefing him properly — is this claim fair?
- What is good practice?
- What is your role as the boy's year head and where do you fit in to the total picture?

What is the school's position in this case and what is the role of the year head?

Schools are busy places, and teachers are often burdened with so many responsibilities that they get little time to stand back from any situation and assess it objectively. All too frequently, they do not notice things that, given the time to reflect, should have been obvious. In this case the boy was demonstrating symptoms that all was not well for some time before he was found wandering the streets. The tutor's claim that he should have been better informed partially reflects his feelings of guilt about the symptoms he observed in Derrick's behaviour, about which he failed to take any action. He also wants to avoid blame. It is also the case that teachers consistently ask what signs should they watch for, almost as if they expect there to be a checklist of signs, and, of course, it is not as simple as this.

Clarify the position

First of all, clarify the position for the tutor. Since the Hunt Report of 1994 (DfEE 1994), schools have tried hard to ensure that they carry out their responsibilities for child protection properly and in a way that will not lead to public censure. This report followed a highly publicised incident, and focused on how abuse should have been prevented or detected earlier and how the school and the LEA responded to the complaints, once raised. It was generally critical of the school's awareness of child-protection issues. In the school concerned there was not only unawareness but also a general unwillingness to believe that such a thing was possible, and children were not listened to. The report was even more critical of how the case was handled by the school, because it considered that a member of staff went too far in investigating the case personally rather than handing it over to the child-protection agency. It was also extremely critical of the way that the LEA handled the case once it became public.

Reassure the tutor

You can give the tutor some reassurance. This is important because he is clearly feeling both anxious and guilty. Putting the incident into perspective will help the tutor, as well as repairing relations between you. In Case Study 10.3 there has been no serious neglect of duty; rather the school has been a bit slow in putting two and two together. The school failed to pick up on some symptoms of distress. Had the tutor thought to tell you about the symptoms that he observed, you could have begun to consult the relevant agencies and put processes into play, which could have helped the pupil. Nevertheless, you should be grateful that the tutor did not try to press the child to talk to him because, if this had been mishandled, it could have created very serious problems later on both for the investigation of the pupil's statement and any case that may be brought.

You can also reassure the tutor that he is not expected to be an expert on child abuse. The school must have a child-protection policy and this should be readily available for staff to consult should the need arise. Make a point of telling your whole tutor team to familiarize themselves with the contents of this document and to consult the school's named person about any points which are unclear. Not knowing what the policy says, or worse still where it is, can leave the year team open to criticism. In the school involved in the case referred to in the Hunt inquiry only one person actually knew where the policy was.

Tutors are often anxious that they won't recognize the signs of abuse. An exemplar describing the main categories of abuse and how to recognize them may be found in Case Study 10.4. If you use it, emphasize that teachers are not, however, expected to be experts at diagnosis. In Case Study 10.3 there were no clear symptoms by which a tutor could identify sexual abuse, rather there were symptoms of distress and anxiety and some deterioration in the pupil's concentration. They are, however, expected to be vigilant and to refer upwards any worrying signs that they notice. Not seeking help may be a significant indicator of a teacher, or a school, which is underprepared.

Make it clear what should be done in future

As a team you should learn from this incident. Providing clear guidelines about what your tutors should do if a child-protection issue arises is an essential part of your role as a pastoral team leader. Use a team meeting or INSET session to go through the issues and the procedure with the team, and provide a brief checklist for them to refer to when a problem arises. The checklist could be used as the basis for an INSET session with your team.

Respond positively to the request for training

If your tutor team would like some INSET, provide something that will help them generally in developing their tutoring skills, as well as providing information about child-protection issues (e.g. you could help your tutors develop their listening skills, either by leading a session personally or by booking someone who can provide this). You may want to lead the INSET yourself, but use externally produced materials to focus the session. There are sufficient materials available for this purpose, but you want to ensure that what you use for the session is good, as well as up to date in terms of legal/factual information. The most straightforward way to approach organizing an INSET session is to consult the person responsible for child protection in your school and ask him/her for a list of up-to-date, quality materials.

Emphasize the need for vigilance

What is really essential is that tutors are vigilant for any signs of distress, or changes in the behaviour or attitude of the pupils in their tutor group. The child may not be exhibiting symptoms of child abuse at all – something quite different may be wrong. What really matters is that the child's signals meet with a response. In Case Study 10.3 the pupil did not try to talk to the tutor or to any other member of staff. Adolescents find it much more difficult than young children to share such intimate personal information. Their feelings of shame and embarrassment can make it difficult for them to confide in a teacher. Confidences should never be forced. In Derrick's case, however, by lingering in the classroom after school, even though he did not talk about his problems, he was giving out signals that all was not well, and that some help was needed. Perhaps if the tutor had started to chat to him, Derrick might have gained sufficient confidence to begin to confide in him.

Stress the importance of listening sensitively to pupils who want to talk or confide

It is important that the pupil is given an opportunity to talk to someone to whom s/he can relate. Encourage your tutor team to listen sensitively if a pupil wants to talk to them. When a pupil begins to talk about his/her problem, whatever it is, the tutors will not know what might lie ahead. Your advice to your tutor team should be that they should not ask too many questions, or press for disclosures. What they should do is to give the pupil the space to talk, and help the child to feel safe and to feel that the teacher will know what to do. They should not interrupt or disturb the flow. It is particularly important that an overconscientious teacher does not put the subsequent investigation or a court hearing at risk by asking questions which could put ideas into a child's mind. '*Did he tell you to touch him?*' or '*Does Dad hit you often?*' are clear examples of leading questions; whereas '*That's a nasty bruise, how did it happen?*' is a more open question, which provides an opportunity for the pupil to confide. It must be the child's story with no grounds for anyone to claim afterwards that the child was coached into providing particular details in the story.

If you want to sum up this advice for your tutors, TACADE's 'caring' principle is a useful mnemonic. It is also relevant when children want to tell you about bullying issues (see Chapter 8):

- create a warm supportive atmosphere;
- allow children to express strong feelings;
- reflect back and respond appropriately;
- investigate the situation sensitively, remembering not to take the investigation too far;

- negotiate a way forward with the child;
- go forward, learning from mistakes, planning carefully.

Make a record of what is said

The task of the tutor is to listen, gather information and make a record of what was said and pass this upwards. The record is important because a case may not come to court for a long time, and accuracy in giving evidence is vital. In exceptional cases, the person who first hears the child's story may be required to give evidence and this could be as long as a year later. Remind your tutors that they can never promise confidentiality to a pupil. It is important to make it clear to pupils that any discussion cannot be confidential and that parts of it may have to be passed on to a third party. They must always set these parameters in advance.

Always consult about referral

It is not always clear-cut that the child is reporting abuse, so encourage your tutors to consult you if there is a doubt about what the problem is. In fact, it is very important that the tutor refers the problem upwards immediately a serious issue arises. The decision about whether to refer should be taken by someone senior, preferably a decision will be taken jointly by you and the person named as responsible for child-protection issues. It is not unlikely that the head teacher will also be consulted. Even if you decide not to refer the problem, you still need documentation. It is important to record, for example, that you have decided to continue to monitor the situation. Schools were worried after the Hunt Report that deciding to do nothing could count against them later, so they did not record the incidents, but hid them. My clear advice is that this is not a wise strategy; rather, you should record the incident and the decision reached, together with the reasons for the decision, and that you should include the statement that you will continue to monitor the situation. Make sure also that the statement/report is witnessed. This also saves muddle or any confusion later on.

Clarify who should handle the referral

If it is clearly a child-abuse problem, then in most cases the tutor should go straight to the person named for child-protection matters. The tutor should inform you next, but the deputy, or whoever the named person is, will need to ring the Child Protection Agency immediately, and it is important that no time is lost, as the agency may wish to take action before the end of the school day. It does not, however, always have to be the named person who makes the initial contact, as sometimes it is useful for the agency to speak to someone who knows the child. What matters is that the procedure is clear to everyone involved and that it is followed, so if you are going to make the contact, this should be agreed with the named person.

How to make a referral – some guidelines

A referral is usually made over the telephone and confirmed in writing. It must contain certain basic information:

- the child's full name, date of birth, address, ethnic and religious group;
- details of other members of the child's family and those who live with them;
- details of all those with parental responsibility, as defined by the Children's Act of 1989, including anyone who lives apart from the child;
- name and phone number of the child's GP and other known medical information;
- whether there are any court orders pertaining to the child, or if the child is already known to social services;
- the whereabouts of the child at the time of the referral and how long the child will be at that place;
- the whereabouts of the parent/s (if known);
- how they can make contact with you for the next few hours;
- a concise description of the child's injuries or allegations;
- any other information requested by the agency.

If possible, contact the agency early enough in the day for the social workers to be able to act on your information during that day. If the child is safe at school for several hours, the social workers/police can start dealing with the case, without the added complication of having to provide for the child's safety. It becomes harder if the child has already gone home from school.

Do not consult the parents at this stage

Although Department of Health guidance wanted the school to contact the parents before making the referral, in practice this is not a viable option and it does not make sense, as the parent/s are likely to want to stop you, and could hide or destroy evidence. It also conflicts with the instruction to ensure that parents are not tipped off prior to an investigation.

Explain the child-protection process

It may be helpful for your team to understand what happens after a referral is made. Basically an investigation has to be carried out, under section 4.7 of the Children's Act, in response to the referral. It has several functions:

- to establish the facts about the situation which has given rise to the referral;
- to make a clear record of the allegations which are being made – what abuse occurred, over what period, etc.?;
- to make an assessment of the current risk to the child;
- to establish whether there are continuing grounds for concern (i.e. whether protection procedures should be invoked).

This is the beginning of the investigative process, and at this stage the primary concern is not to identify the alleged abuser, rather it is to clarify the situation and assess the ongoing risk to the child and of other children living in the household. The process will involve collecting and collating as much information as possible about the child and the family. Each of the agencies involved with the child or the family will be required to contribute and there may be a joint strategy meeting between the key professionals at some point in the process (e.g. to decide whether to move the child out of the home).

If the allegation involves a member of staff the school is obviously much more involved, but, in such cases, senior management will handle the process and your role will be to provide any information that you have that could be relevant.

Interviews with the child should not take place on school premises

There are good reasons for this. Data collected by the social services clearly indicates that children dislike being interviewed at school, even when this is the place in which they first disclosed the abuse. They tend to feel that they have lost their privacy and that everyone knows about the case. Parents also resent the school being involved. If the pupil is to continue at school, it should be a place which is not linked in his/her mind with out-of-school problems.

Provide a secure and caring environment for the pupil

The pupil is experiencing a very difficult and traumatic time. You must settle the pupil back to his/her studies and provide any necessary in-school support. The pupil's behaviour may be affected by what is happening and you may also have to provide guidance for the form tutor to help him support the pupil in an appropriate manner.

Check the PSHE programme

You should be providing opportunities in your year PSHE programme for pupils to explore the issue of abuse. If a situation involving abuse emerges during the year, however, you should check your programme to ensure that it is sensitive enough and will not cause distress to a pupil involved in an investigation, or who has been placed on the child-protection register.

Monitor the situation

One of your main responsibilities, as the year head, is to ensure that those who need to know that the pupil is now on the register have been informed, and that they understand what this means. You should monitor the child's behaviour and progress, both to check how the child is coping and because you may be asked for follow up information. Keep clear records of the pupil's progress in a secure location, so that you have no problems in producing reports for case conferences and make sure that you, or the responsible person, do attend to represent the school at any conferences which are held.

Maintain good liaison with the relevant agencies

Efficient transfer of necessary information is almost always one of the weak links in the system. Social services are responsible for informing schools that a pupil has been placed on the child-protection register, but information often trickles through slowly and lags behind events. Schools always grumble about the difficulty of contacting social workers or the psychological services. Schools in turn are sometimes slow about providing information either to social services or to the school to which a pupil has been transferred. Information about pupils going on or off the register is often co-ordinated by the Education Welfare Service, and one of the things you should clarify is what to do if the pupil is absent.

CASE STUDY 10.4

Exemplar of a definition of abuse for use with your tutor team

WHAT IS MEANT BY CHILD ABUSE

A definition of abuse

Injury, neglect or harm – either physical, emotional or sexual – which is caused to a child by his/her parents or carer, either by deliberate acts or by failure to protect them.

Main categories of abuse

Physical injury

This includes bruises, lacerations, burns, fractures, eye injuries, etc. All children are liable to cuts and bruises from time to time and it can be difficult to distinguish between accidental injuries and abuse. This makes teachers very wary of suggesting that a child may be suffering abuse. If you do notice bruising or other injuries, keep an eye on the frequency that the injuries occur and whether they are always to the same parts of the body. Notice also if the marks look like the outline of an instrument such as a stick or brush, or the bruising is on fleshy areas such as the upper thighs or arms, or the child has burn/scorch marks (e.g. on hands or feet).

Neglect/failure to thrive

You may notice that a member of your tutor group is poorly clothed, dirty or frequently hungry when he/she arrives at school. The procedure in this case of possible neglect is different from other incidents of abuse. The logical person to mention this to is the school nurse, who will be able to apply objective criteria such as growth milestones, or the head of year, who can liaise with the Education Welfare Officer, who carries out home visits in the course of her duties.

Emotional abuse

Unless a pupil confides in you directly, you are unlikely to be able to identify emotional abuse; rather, you may find that a pupil has very low self-esteem, but you do not know why this is the case. Sometimes this causes the pupil to behave badly and be difficult to teach; at other times it has the effect of making the child over-anxious to please because s/he is afraid of displeasing adults. Such pupils may also be very clingy and want a lot of your time and attention. Occasionally (e.g. in a PSHE lesson), they may speak of what they are experiencing at home.

Sexual abuse

Sexual abuse includes touching, penetration and other sexual acts and requiring children to behave sexually, act as a source of adult sexual stimulation or participate in experiences which are inappropriate for children. It can also include exposure to pornography, and usually involves 'grooming' (i.e. preparation for the abuse), rather than being a spur-of-the-moment incident. Signs of sexual abuse range from a general mistrust of adults to gross physical injury or pain in the genital area.

At risk of abuse

The concept of 'dangerousness', identifying whether a child is at risk, is actually the key issue in determining whether a child should be placed on the child-protection register. A child's confidences may lead you to think that s/he is at risk. You have to inform the deputy who will consult the professionals, whose job it is to do a risk analysis.

Your responsibility as a tutor

In all cases in which you think you have noticed any of the signs of abuse mentioned above, it is your duty immediately to inform either your head of year or the pastoral deputy, who holds responsibility for child protection.

Liaising with the Psychological Services

CASE STUDY 10.5

For action

You are head of year 8. The head of art finds you at break to have a word with you. She is concerned because recently the imagery and colours that Jamie uses in his painting have altered starkly. '*I had begun to notice that he was using very dark colours and that some of the images are quite violent, then we did a family scene*', she says. '*Jamie's painting is black and there is a very small father figure, just on the edge of the picture. Is he having problems at home?*' she asks, '*and is it affecting the rest of his work?*'

For discussion

This is the first indication that Jamie is experiencing family difficulty. As Jamie's year head, what action should you take?

Art is one area in which pupils express feelings and emotions that they may be experiencing, but that they find hard to discuss orally. It can, however, be difficult for teachers to interpret the message the pupil is trying to convey. What signs should you look for and what should you do when a pupil's work in art, or essays in English, contain signs of inner turmoil?

This is an area in which you may wish to seek advice from the school psychological service, not merely to learn what to look out for, but also what the boundaries of your role are. A teacher, who acts like a social worker, deprives the pupil of the expert help to which s/he is entitled. We have to know our limits. Enthusiastic amateurs, who for the best of reasons and particularly because they care about the pupils for whom they are responsible want to sort the matter out, are often reluctant to hand the matter over to some other professional, whose actions and decisions they cannot control. Their responsibility to the child and concern for his/her best interests actually means that they should consult. Doing the job well includes not undoing someone else's.

Case Study 10.6 is an example of the kind of welfare issue which really needs expert care.

CASE STUDY 10.6

For action/discussion – Cutting

Cuts are noticed by the pupil's friends, who consult you

You are the head of year 11. Sally's friends come to see you because they are very worried about her. They have noticed that when she changes for PE, there are scars not only on her arms but also on her stomach. When they asked her about the scars she made excuses, and since then has tried to avoid taking part in PE or changing where they can see her. They suspect that she has been cutting herself on a regular basis. They say that she is one of the brightest pupils in the form with no academic problems, but since the summer holiday she has become very withdrawn, even with them, and seems to have little confidence. They think it is more than the approach of GCSE. Sally has never been seriously worried about examinations before and always does well. They have come to you because she will not confide in them.

Assessing the problem

You take a look at Sally in assembly and about the school and you notice that she is extremely thin, much thinner than you remember her being earlier in the year. This raises concerns about possible anorexia as well as cutting. You know that these problems often go together. Talking to Sally is not very productive. She keeps insisting that everything is 'all right', but clearly it is not. It is going to take a lot of sensitive counselling before Sally will be prepared to talk. You are reluctant to undertake this because you are beginning to suspect that there may be a really serious problem, which may take more skill than you have. You also think that there is a definite start date for this problem, whatever it is. Before the holiday Sally was her normal self, since the summer holiday, however, a series of symptoms have emerged.

Consulting the parents

You decide to have a word with Sally's mother, who is aware that her daughter is losing weight, but is not aware of any scars. Sally's mother becomes very anxious. She trusts you and wants to use you as a counsellor, but you are already beginning to feel that Sally really needs help from the psychological service. You suggest that a possible course of action could be to take Sally for a general medical check-up, using the weight loss as an excuse. That way there is no need for Sally to know that the school has been in touch with the family. The family doctor, who has known Sally since she was a small child, could be briefed in advance. You think that Sally's cutting is an urgent plea for help and, if her mother uses the route you suggest, the doctor could deal with any medical issues and make the necessary recommendation for educational psychological services to become involved in the case. Once this recommendation has been made, you can liaise with the educational psychologist as necessary on a need-to-know basis, while the outside agencies manage the problem.

Sally is reluctant to go to the doctor, and continues to claim that nothing is wrong. Her mother is now very worried because Sally is eating very little and she catches Sally making herself sick after a family meal. This gives her the excuse to insist on taking Sally to see the doctor, and she is appalled when the doctor's examination reveals just how badly her daughter is cutting herself. The psychological service is now brought into the case.

As usual, however, there is a time lag before Sally's first appointment with the educational psychologist, and a week later there is a development in the case. Sally has continued to cut herself, and the cuts begin to bleed badly. Sally has to be removed from her lesson and is brought to your office weeping. At this point you feel that you could probably get Sally to talk, but you resist the temptation. This case is outside your area of expertise and should be handled by professionals. You consult your line manager, the pastoral deputy, who confirms your opinion, and then you ring Sally's mother and ask her to come and collect her daughter, who is not in a fit state to attend school.

It is also very unsettling for other students, and you may find that you have to support other members of the form. Sally's friends, who are very upset about what is happening to Sally, come to see you at lunchtime. Providing support and reassurance for Sally's friends and helping them to cope with what has happened to her is one of your responsibilities as year head. They need the opportunity to talk through their feelings and any reassurance you can give them. You provide them with the address of the local 'Way-In Centre' so that, if they feel they would like further counselling with an outsider, they can easily access it. You can also discuss with them how they can help Sally without becoming overinvolved, especially as for, a while, they may not be able to visit her. One way is to write cheerful friendly notes to her while she is at home.

Often the act of cutting produces copycat followers, and, although these incidents are usually not as serious as the original one, you should monitor the form closely in the weeks that follow to check that you do not have an outbreak of cutting on your hands. Generally, if the cutting has spread to other pupils, other members of the form or year group come to tell you. The 'copycat' normally has problems of her own, and wants attention. In this case, Sally's friend, Nerissa, did start to cut her arms, but her case was much easier for you to deal with because Nerissa was actually keen to talk to you about her home problems as well as her anxiety both about her school work and about Sally. Again, after consultation with the pupil's family, your help is supplemented by some sessions with the school counsellor, and Nerissa, who has felt abandoned during a difficult time for the family, begins to feel more valued at home and her progress in class steadily improves.

Sally, however, has to be hospitalized for a while and teaching has to be arranged for her while she is in the hospital. In this case, to everyone's relief, there is a positive outcome and Sally is able to return to school a few months later. Her friends continue to support her and write regularly to her in hospital, and, before Sally comes back to school, you have another session with them, at their request, to help them handle her re-entry.

In this case study, although you may have strong suspicions, you never learn what the problem actually is. As the year leader, your responsibility is to ensure that the pupil receives the best possible help from the appropriate agency, not to deal with all aspects of it personally. You are also responsible for helping the pupil's friends understand and cope with the situation, especially as, as sometimes happens, there is no positive outcome and the pupil is not able to resume full-time education.

For discussion

- What are the issues involved in the case study?
- How does this case study compare with your own experience?

BIBLIOGRAPHY AND FURTHER READING

Brown, D. (1995) *Responding to Child Abuse*, Community Education Development Centre publication, London: Bedford Square Press.

Mental Health Foundation (1999) *Bright Futures Report*, London: Mental Health Foundation.

DfEE (1994) *The Protection of Children from Abuse*, Circular 10/95, London: HMSO. (The Report of the Hunt Committee).

DfEE (1994) *Pupils with Problems*, A collection of DfE Circulars 8/94 and 9/94, London: HMSO.

The Advisory Council on Alcohol and Drug Education (TACADE) (1990) *Skills for the Primary Child*, London: TACADE (dated but still very useful).

Webb, S. (1994) *Troubled and Vulnerable Children, a Practical Guide for Heads*, Kingston upon Thames: Croner Publications Ltd.

Whitney, B. (1994) *The Children's Act and Schools*, London: Kogan Page.

Whitney, B. (1996) *Child Protection for Teachers and Schools*, London: Kogan Page.

Wonnacott, J. (1995) *Protecting children in school*, A handbook for developing child-protection training, London: National Children's Bureau.

Chapter 11

Your role in raising pupil attainment

What is your role in helping the pupil raise his/her achievement? This chapter will describe different approaches which schools have used to raise pupil attainment, and discuss the role of the pastoral leader in raising standards.

A lot of the case studies are for reflection. They are included to enable you to benchmark against your own school's practice and to give an indication of the range of schemes aimed at raising pupil attainment currently being used in schools. Where possible I have included schemes that have been up and running for long enough for the school to have reviewed and revised them in the light of their experience, but there are also descriptions of some schemes which are still in pilot stage. This device is used to help you in your role as a manager and innovator – you can reflect on how the innovation is being introduced, as well as what it is.

The current emphasis on raising achievements is political, but nevertheless it is what schools are about. The thrust towards raising achievement has brought about a change of emphasis in your role as a pastoral manager. Your responsibilities have also expanded and now cover three main areas of the pupil's schooling:

1. *providing a positive environment for learning* – this means providing a secure environment in which the pupil is able to concentrate on his/her studies;
2. *managing the learning programme for the pupils* – you co-ordinate the pupil's studies and act as the director of studies for the pupils in your year group or house;
3. *monitoring pupil progress through use of the available data and setting targets with the pupils.*

CREATING A SECURE LEARNING ENVIRONMENT

The tragic events of the last few years have, quite rightly, led many schools to bring safety and the security of the children and the staff right up their list of priorities. In this chapter, however, what I want to address is the issue of the various ways in which you can provide the secure, yet stimulating, working atmosphere which is essential for creating a climate of achievement. It is a major part of your responsibilities to provide for the pupils within your year group or house a working environment which enables them to achieve their potential. You may or may not be able to do much about the actual conditions in which they have to study, but you can do a lot about creating an ethos which will help them achieve.

Many of you will have responsibility to support and encourage pupils who do not come from a background which facilitates study. You have to think about how to motivate these pupils and help them persevere when the going gets difficult. Case Studies 11.7 and 11.8 describe strategies adopted by schools who have had to tackle this issue.

At the opposite extreme, you may be a head of a year, or of a house in a school, in which the academic pressures to succeed are intense. You will have to give thought as to how to enable the students to cope with the pressures and stresses both within school and at home. You may want to revisit some of the case studies included in Chapters 9 and 10 in terms of helping these pupils achieve their potential.

CASE STUDY 11.1

For reflection

Some questions to think about

The answers may be different in each school, but providing answers is vital to your success in helping your students. Some of the strategies described in the case studies which follow indicate how these questions have been answered in particular schools.

1. How do you enable pupils to feel safe in working hard without being taunted by their peers and labelled, for example, as 'swots' or sad?
2. How do you help pupils to have the confidence to answer questions or put forward ideas in class without fear of ridicule from teachers or from other pupils?
3. How do you encourage pupils to 'have a go' at a new or difficult technique, or to feel that they can take risks without worrying too much about possible failure?
4. How do you encourage pupils to have the confidence to say 'I need help' or 'I can't see how to do this'. This can occur at both ends of the academic spectrum.
5. How do you help students to be able to say 'No' to those peers who are distractors and who waste their own and everyone else's time in class?
6. How do you use your tutorial time or your Personal, Social and Health Education (PSHE) programme to help pupils to begin to feel 'I can do it!' rather than 'It's no good trying, I can't do it'.

MANAGING THE LEARNING PROGRAMME FOR THE PUPILS

Providing a comfortable, creative, pleasant working environment will also entail working closely with the subject leaders. High-quality pastoral support should complement and support good classroom teaching. Managing this partnership effectively is one of the real tests you face as a pastoral manager. Your role is to monitor the learning programme for each student and provide appropriate overall direction, suggestions and encouragement. Whether it is a year group or a house, you are the 'director of studies' for your section. The subject leader is responsible for the pupil's progress within that subject. At times the subject teacher may get this out of proportion and you may have to intervene, either directly or via the subject leader, in order that the overall programme is manageable. At other times the subject leader or a subject teacher may come to you, because s/he has some concerns about the pupil's progress (e.g. s/he thinks that a pupil is underperforming in the subject).

One particularly sensitive area is how do you persuade some teachers to respond more positively to the pupils' needs? For example, how do you persuade those who disparage, or who answer a request for help with the accusation that the pupil hasn't listened and the implication that it is the pupil's fault that s/he doesn't understand, to change their approach? This is generally best approached through the management of the school's teaching and learning strategies, but even then a few teachers will be very resistant to changing their teaching style. Because the problem is located outside your area of authority you would be well advised to refer it to your line manager or the teachers' line managers. This is certainly the case if the insensitive teacher is a head of department (HoD) or faculty. An example of this kind is described in Chapter 7 'Managing the partnership with parents'. You can support the pupils, however, by using tutorial time to help them develop coping strategies to manage in these lessons.

Some schools manage the liaison between the subject and pastoral areas very well, others are less well developed. In Case Study 11.2 the system is basically in place.

CASE STUDY 11.2

Communication between subject teacher and the tutor

Referral form

Name: *Anne-Louise Simpson*   Tutor group: *8G*   Tutor:

M.G.

Date: Department: *Mod. Languages*

Location: Please mark with X

Lesson X/Registration /Assembly /Dining hall /Corridors /Outside /Other please specify

Achievements		Problems	
Improved work/ behaviour	Good attitude	Unwilling to work	Distracts others

Improved punctuality	Consistently good homework	Persistent lateness	Homework not completed
Working well in groups/with others	Shows initiative	Aggressive/ threatening behaviour to others	*Does not meet deadlines* X
Positive attitude	Well organized	Truancy	Does not bring equipment to lessons
Gives positive lead to others	Improved effort	Racist or sexist remarks	Disobedience
High-quality coursework	Good test scores	Rudeness	*Easily distracted* X
Excellent overall performance	Helpful in class	Noisy in class	Does not persevere

Other information:

Action taken: *I have spoken two or three times recently to Anne-Louise about her failure to give in assignments on time, but she always has an excuse. Is this happening in her other subjects or does she just lack commitment in my subject? Increasingly recently she is easily distracted and looks for excuses to come off task.*

Further action needed: Subject: *I will continue to monitor and liaise with you.*

Further action needed: Pastoral: *Investigate. See if you can have more effect than I can!*

Initials: *F.B.*   Date: *12.2*

Source: Powell (1997).

For discussion

- How should the tutor deal with this communication?
- What is your role in supporting the tutor?

A range of strategies will be needed to help the pupils achieve their potential. All schools are different, and strategies which will be effective in some schools will not work in others, but what really matters is that within a school you all pull together and give to the pupils the same message. This requires good liaison, and understanding and respect for boundaries.

UNDERSTANDING WHAT RAISES ATTAINMENT

Understanding what raises achievement is essential to achieving your aim, because it will help you and your colleagues decide how to approach your responsibilities and to work out an appropriate strategy or range of strategies.

CASE STUDY 11.3

For reflection

Comparing two ways of viewing this issue

Note both the similarities and the differences in these two approaches. You can use them as a checklist against which you can evaluate your own practice. This material could also be used for an in-service education and training (INSET) session for the year/house leaders, and as the basis for planning a pastoral thrust on raising pupil achievement.

A What raises attainment?

This list is based on material used by the Haringey Education Service. In a school in which attainment is improving:

- the school's key purpose is education;
- the children know that they are in school to learn;
- the whole ethos of the school is learning centred;
- there is clear communication with and between staff, children and parents;
- the teachers build on the pupils' previous experiences;
- starting points are appropriate;
- clear targets are set matched carefully to the pupils' needs;
- timescales and success criteria are appropriate;
- goals are achievable – within the pupil's extended grasp;

- both the children and the teachers know when progress is or is not being made;
- interest, specific praise and encouragement are used effectively;
- firmness and support are used effectively to encourage the pupils to stay on task;
- the pupils can rely on appropriate help to put things right or get better;
- manageable and useful records/data are kept and used;
- all involved learn from mistakes – learning from mistakes becomes part of the learning experience;
- continuity is maintained – from day to day, and year to year;
- appropriate progression opportunities are provided;
- the pupils increase in confidence and self-esteem.

B *Creating an ethos of achievement (George 1997):*

1. all pupils know they are valued and cared for;
2. teamwork ethos is fostered;
3. celebration of successes – academic, sporting, drama, caring, etc. – through assemblies, tutor groups, commendations, letters home, etc.;
4. emphasis on the $+$ and $-$ becomes suppressed;
5. good attendance rewarded, pupils value coming to school, school gives them something and leaves them wanting more;
6. Enrichment of the curriculum by extra-curricular activities (pupils have lots of opportunities outside the classroom – if they know about them);
7. valued rewards system;
8. pupils given responsibility at home and at school;
9. pupils contribute to the development of the school (e.g. School Council, prefects?);
10. winning competitions – local and national;
11. sense of identity and purpose – school well led (parents, staff and pupils informed and consulted, whole-team approach, parents good role models);
12. take risks – make it work!;
13. have systems in place to recognize underachievement (monitoring) – encouragement;
14. environment – comfortable, creative, pleasant working environment;
15. pupils are trusted (excellent relationships between pupils and staff).

CASE STUDY 11.4

For reflection or for discussion

The rewards system

'We are moving this school forward and encouraging the pupils to want to raise their achievement by the use of a whole range of rewards ...' A headteacher explains her favoured approach to raising achievement.

One method currently being used, which started from a very low attainment level, is to encourage pupils to want to improve their performance by using a reward system. It targets the issue of labelling the hard-working pupil as 'sad' or the odd person out, and aims at creating an ethos in which it is 'in' to attend and work. The examples of this approach, which follow, illustrate ways in which different schools have applied the approach.

River View Community School

Year-11 attendance initiative – our development plan

Rationale for the initiative

Attendance is a particular problem for us. By year 11 attendance is way below the 90 per cent standard set by Ofsted, and the parents generally condone their children's absence. We believe that this has a devastating effect on the progress made by our pupils and on our GCSE results. If we could improve attendance in year 11 our pupils would have a much better chance of securing their GCSEs.

Target – hard objective

Our target is to get pupils to want to improve their attendance in year 11. Providing a fun, yet purposeful way of improving attendance is the basis of our plan for a pilot scheme to see whether it will work. It is linked to the school development plan about raising standards of achievement and is called 'Hard Target 1'.

Done	Task no.	Hard targets/ objectives	How? action, soft targets	By whom	Start date	Revised date	End date	Resources, time, meetings, Training	Cost	Desired outcomes
	3	Improve Y11 attendance	Staff discuss initiative with pupils	HoY tune tutors	10th January		3 weeks	Year team meeting, info sheet	Trivial ca. £10 per year for books of cloakroom tickets and 100% stickers	Improved and sustained good attendance
			Form tutors issue initialled cloakroom	Form tutors	1st February			Year meeting Form time – for issuing		Impact on progress – contributes to raising

			tickets weekly to students with 100% attendance				tickets		achievement
			Attach 100% stickers to planners						
			Raffle draw at end of term	HoY – at year assessment		Review first cycle	Last week of term		Cost of prizes
			Present prizes						

For discussion

Is this scheme likely to achieve its objective in (1) the short term, (2) the long term?
   What factors should you take into account when planning this type of initiative?
   What kind of prizes would be suitable?
   Are there other issues that you should keep in mind when considering a reward system?

Hillside School

A head of house describes the changes in attitude at her school following the introduction of a house reward system:

For us, the trigger was the introduction of a house system which enabled vertical social mixing. Contests and competitions were introduced. We felt that the children needed something to be involved in, something where they could win awards. They wanted to try hard for each other. The house system has had a tremendous impact. It was as if the pupils suddenly started to believe in themselves. The following term, we souped up the reward system and linked it into the house system and then we built in a good work assembly. Now good work is rewarded with house points, and, if a pupil earns ten house points, s/he receives a SMART [specific, measurable, achievable, resourced, time-related] certificate at the regular Monday good-work assembly. Exceptional total scores are rewarded with something that the pupils will enjoy (e.g. a free gym or swimming at the local sports centre). Termly, totals go towards awards which we present at the end-of-term assembly. At these events the children may be presented with pencils, book tokens, sports bags, mugs and rulers stamped with the school logo.

Certificates are certainly not handed out easily; the children have to work really hard to earn the points. Nor are we handing out certificates to unruly pupils in the hope that they will sit down and work; discipline in the school is tight. If there are problems with a pupil, we have established a system in which the tutor will have a meeting with the pupil, and they set targets together. Everything is recorded in a planner. Each child has his/her personal planner which is checked regularly by the tutor. Parents are called into the school and involved in the process. If these measures don't work, the pupil spends a day out of class, working alone, supervised by a senior member of staff. We don't have to do this often. Rewards far outnumber sanctions.

We can see a real difference in the children's attitude. They have got into the habit of working hard and applying themselves in class. It wasn't an overnight sensation, more of a gradual process, but I do remember walking along a corridor a few months after we had intro-duced the scheme, and being surprised to see the level of concentration in the classrooms. It didn't used to be like that. There have also been spin-offs in how the children conduct them-selves around the school. There is much less tension, and they seem to treat each other and the building with more respect. We can put displays up now and expect them to survive. Now it is the small number of pupils who aren't working who are out of step. It is 'in' to be involved and working and everyone wants to belong to the in-crowd.

The reward system is having an effect on the pupils' self-esteem. It was really low at the start of the project. Our pupils saw themselves as failures. We have worked hard to make them believe in themselves and to expect well of themselves. The rewards system is a means to an end. We have raised the game for our pupils. We are not a top school yet, far from it, but the number of pupils achieving A–Cs at GCSE went up substantially this year and we want to maintain this momentum.

For discussion

1. Compare this system with assertive discipline described in Chapter 8.
2. In both schools the tutor is the linchpin. How do you ensure commitment from your tutor team?
3. Some schools have received a bad press for the use of rewards, particularly those which use cash prizes. What are the issues involved here and how can they be resolved? Has Hillside School managed to do so?
4. There are far more elements here than just a rewards system – what are they and how are they meshed together?
5. Case Study 11.7 (see p. 182) discusses how Westlea High School had to adapt and modify its academic tutoring system in order to maintain the momentum of raising standards. What are the implications for Hillside School (described in Case Study 11.4)?

CASE STUDY 11.5

For reflection

Using weekly planners – Marley High School

The weekly planners are used really effectively. The parents, who make occasional comments or suggestions regularly, sign them, and there are plenty of tutors' comments. The tutors reply when the parents ask something, and there seems to be a real dialogue. The tutors' comments are concise but helpful. They encourage, praise improvement and give concise advice. They move pupils on by making sensible and realistic suggestions about what they can do next. Sometimes the pupil writes a question in the summary section. A child told me that he only writes like this if he is afraid that he might forget what he wants to ask, or to record the decision. Mainly, the pupils record their homework and other things they have to do, with the date to give the work in, but they also use a tick system to record completed tasks or assignment. I have rarely seen a school use the planners as effectively as this. In many schools the planners exist in name only. I rarely see them being used in tutor time or at the end of lessons and there are often huge gaps in entries. In this school in every lesson the pupils write their homework into the planner. It is so engrained that few subject teachers have to remind the pupils to use the planners.

(An inspector enthuses about the use of weekly planners in Marley High School)

CASE STUDY 11.6

For reflection

Making use of the community

1 Highcrest High School

We wanted to support the pupils without making any additional demands on our staff, so we involved the community. Retired volunteers from Age Concern help us in a number of ways. In one of the initiatives they help on a one-to-one basis with literacy skills. Our year-7 pupils arrive in the school with very underdeveloped literacy, and a major thrust in year 7 is to improve their skills. I have to train the volunteers and manage the system, but I consider that it is time well spent. In the mid- and end-of-year tests and assessments, literacy is considerably improved and the pupils are able to cope with their National Curriculum programme. The volunteers become very involved in the project, enjoy the work and develop a good relationship with the pupils. They are also involved in family reading – helping parents to read with their children – and with running the homework clubs for Key Stage 3 pupils.

2 Downtown High School

Our reading volunteer scheme

We were really pleased when, as a result of our involvement in the local Education Business Partnership, a link was set up with a leading law firm. I was asked to co-ordinate it. The firm's representative asked what assistance the school most needed, and I said that it was help with our literacy initiative. It is an inner-city school and the children arrive in school at least 2 years, and often more, behind their chronological reading age. The firm took a while to think about the problem, and then offered to provide twenty volunteers each week to read with the year-7 pupils at lunchtime. We promptly accepted this offer and the scheme started after half-term. An initial training session was held at the firm's offices, so that we could brief the volunteers on how to use their time most effectively, and to answer their questions about the school, the pupils or their task. The literacy co-ordinator helped me to deliver this session.

The scheme really took off, and now we have sixty volunteers helping the children. An end-of-year event, held at the firm's offices, was socially successful, and this year we began to develop further links to help us in the library and to support the pupils' social and cultural developments, especially music. Our main feeder school became interested in this initiative, and now a scheme is operating in year 6 at this primary school, which we hope will impact on the literacy level of pupils entering our school.

We are just beginning to monitor systematically the effect on our pupils. There seems to be an effect both in terms of attitude and on their reading age. The gap between their chronological age and their actual reading age narrowed during year 7. Of course, this varied from pupil to pupil, but all made some progress.

Some good relationships developed between the pupils and their helpers, and we have set up a working group of firm/school representatives to consider mentoring certain pupils through their school career.

I personally learned a lot from my involvement in the scheme, and the firm have offered me a place on one of their in-house courses and a work placement for a week towards the end of summer term so that I can develop my interpersonal skills.

For reflection/discussion

Compare the two similar schemes operating in the schools described above.

- How might you use this idea in your own school?
- What are the implications for you as a manager of being involved in or organizing this kind of scheme?

MENTORING

Mentoring, which is sometimes termed 'academic tutoring', is an approach that is often used to help pupils raise their achievement. It is not the same as counselling, which tends to be concerned with the pupil's welfare and involves a pupil talking through a problem in order to move forward or resolve it. Mentoring concentrates on helping the pupil to improve his/her performance in class. It tends to be used at critical times in a student's school career (e.g. in year 11, or sometimes in year 9), and it provides support for the pupil through linking the pupil with an individual, who supervises their progress. The scheme described in Case Study 11.6 is actually a form of mentoring which targets improving literacy in year 7. Usually, however, the mentor is a member of staff, or sometimes it is another pupil. They meet on a regular basis to discuss the pupil's work and progress and to help the pupil to move forward in his/her studies. Its value is that the student is provided with one-to-one support. Case Studies 11.7 and 11.8 describe two initiatives of this kind.

CASE STUDY 11.7

For action/discussion

Academic tutoring

Westlea High School

We introduced academic tutoring into year 11 three years ago. We had the problem that our results were low, only 25 per cent of pupils obtained A–C grades at GCSE. The school is in an area with high unemployment and 65 per cent of the pupils are on free school meals.

Ideally we should have liked to have involved the parents in supporting the pupils, but there was a problem in that either they did not know how to provide appropriate support or they were unwilling to become involved. It would have taken us too long and would have been something of a culture change to have trained them up at this stage, so we had to look for another way through.

We thought long and hard about the problem and eventually decided to provide every year-11 pupil with a member of staff as an academic tutor. Because we are an 11–16 school, we could not involve sixth-formers. We offered the pupils some free choice in selecting their tutor as we felt that they would work best with someone they found sympathetic. Most staff ended up with about four tutees.

The tutor met their tutees on an individual basis about once a fortnight. The pupils were set individual targets and the discussion centred on how they were progressing towards them. A lot of emphasis was put on helping the pupils to produce their coursework within the deadlines, as this is a persistent area of difficulty for us.

Initially there was a good impact on performance. Our pass rate went up from 25 per cent to 32 per cent, but over the next couple of years it seemed to plateau, so we reviewed the system. We were particularly concerned that, although most teachers did not grumble, providing individual tutors for the whole year group made an enormous demand on the staff and we were not sure that this was cost-effective, so this year we changed the system.

We no longer provide every pupil with an individual tutor; rather, we have identified the underachievers using our value-added information, and we have targeted a small group of these pupils. The pupils chosen are not the worst underachievers, they are the ones for whom, on the basis of our knowledge about them after 4 years in the school, we feel that positive intervention could make a real difference.

These pupils receive a 6-week programme. This time we chose the tutors. Eight of us are implementing the programme and the pupils report to us weekly.

We also identified the pupils whose progress was adversely affected by their poor attendance and have specifically targeted this, this time using the form tutors.

The reaction of the pupils to the change in the scheme is interesting in itself. There was considerable disappointment because many had been looking forward to having an individual tutor in year 11. Others, including the lowest achievers, expressed surprise that they are not on the list.

The scheme has been clearly explained to parents and the tutors have contacted each home involved. We would like the parents to help continue the programme after the 6 weeks, but do not expect much of this to happen. Nevertheless, the parents seem pleased that their child is included in the programme.

We felt that we had to use this reaction to benefit the pupils and so we have created a ongoing programme, and another group have now been selected to receive tutor support in the second part of term.

We intend to review the programme after the results are published in the summer and expect to modify the programme in the light of our findings. We are also beginning to look at ways that we can support pupils at the end of Key Stage 3.

(Key Stage 4 co-ordinator discusses the system of academic tutoring which has been adopted in her school)

For discussion

- What are the issues raised by this case study?
- How does the system of academic tutoring implemented in this school compare with your own system?
- If you do not have a system in your school, what are (1) the advantages of having this kind of support for pupils?; (2) the problems involved in setting up and maintaining a system?
- How could you involve parents?
- What other ways could you find to support the pupils learning?

For a sixth-form tutor team

- How would you develop a similar approach in the sixth form?
- In an 11–18 school could you build the form prefects or sixth-formers into this kind of structure?
- How would your sixth-formers benefit from being involved in the scheme? Case Study 11.8 provides answers to these questions.

CASE STUDY 11.8

For action/discussion

Merwick Community School's peer-support initiative

Merwick Community School implemented a system of peer support based on using sixth-formers to help other pupils. The main problem was boys' attainment. Many boys were underachieving and the year heads believed that this was because of their lack of self-discipline combined with low self-esteem. In the programme of strategies, devised by the school to develop the boys' learning skills, they included a mentoring scheme. The mentors were to be sixth-formers – not the most academic pupils, but the ones who could most relate to these pupils because they themselves had been in trouble for not working hard at Key Stages 3 or 4.

We paired the sixth-formers with year-9 pupils who would benefit from support. The pairs were programmed to meet regularly throughout the year. They were encouraged to become friends. The sixth-formers were given some training sessions to help them to get the year-9 pupils to talk about how they behaved in class and their work. The objective was to get them to see it from a new perspective, and to encourage them to be more interested in how they did in their school subjects. Improving their time management was particularly targeted, as we have a problem with completion of coursework within the deadlines.

The year-9 pupils appreciated the time given to them by the older pupils. They were close enough in age to be able to relate well to each other to share experience. When a sixth-former explained the implications of time wasted in the classroom and that mucking about by distracting others or joining in time-wasting activities had affected his own progress and gave clear examples of them, the year-9 pupils listened. One of the areas that they discussed was the negative effect of some of their friendships and of having to be 'one of the boys'. It led the boys themselves to suggest that if the teachers used a seating plan and enforced it firmly, it would give them the excuse not to sit with particular boys who distracted them from working.

We reacted positively to this suggestion, which fitted well with what we had gleaned from the boys' achievement projects, which we were using as benchmarks. We also made available teacher mentors to help pupils who had a particular problem. They could be used when a problem had been identified and year-9 boys requested help. At the beginning, we wondered if this would actually happen, but, as the scheme began to succeed, increasingly it did. Providing small-scale teacher mentoring did not overstretch our staff, but supplemented and supported the scheme. Celebration of success was also carefully worked into the programme.

Once the programme was in place and used consistently, feedback from the year-9 boys was very positive. They said that they liked it because it didn't make them feel exposed or 'sissy' if they took part in the scheme; it did help them and they particularly valued the opportunity to be friends with older boys. Sessions were put into the PSHE programme in which year-9 pupils talked to year-8 pupils about the scheme so that these pupils could look forward to receiving a mentor when they reached year 9.

The sixth-formers also gained from taking part in the scheme because, in order to help the younger pupils, they began to evaluate how they worked and tutors reported some positive effects on their own time management. Pupils who were not 'prefects' and did not usually hold leadership positions in the school were taking responsibility and actively helping other younger pupils. They became very proprietorial towards their 'protégés'. It also gave them a valuable piece of voluntary work to include on their UCAS form and to discuss at interviews. Several said later that the interviewers had been very interested in this part of their sixth-form programme and that it was a topic that they could discuss with confidence. This was particularly useful for us when the scheme came into its second year – the first group spoke to year 12, because they could easily answer the question 'What's in it for us?'

Evaluating the project after the first year we are very pleased with progress so far and are considering how we can build a peer-mentoring scheme into year 11.

For discussion

- What are the gains Merwick Community School derived from this scheme?
- If you do not have a system in your school, what are (1) the advantages of having this kind of support for pupils?, (2) the problems involved in setting up and maintaining a system?
- How difficult/easy was it to implement?

CASE STUDY 11.9

Exemplar, for reflection

Gerrards High School

We stress to the mentors the need to take a positive approach, and try to give them clear advice and guidelines about how to conduct the mentoring sessions.

Guidelines for mentors

- Past failures are to be forgotten and areas of weakness are only mentioned in order to establish a base from which to move forward.
- Tasks should be broken down into a number of steps. There should not be too many steps at any one time. The tasks must be a logical next step for the student and achievable in terms of the pupil's past performance.
- Setbacks should be seen as normal and are not the subject of criticism (i.e. be encouraging, so that the student perseveres when things get difficult).
- Support should be actively given at each stage and the student should be confident that it will be available.
- Current strengths should always be recognized before moving on to learning new skills.
- New achievements should be celebrated. Sometimes sending a pupil to a member of the senior management team (SMT) who has only previously seen the pupil over disciplinary issues can be a very positive experience for the pupil.
- Use your knowledge of the pupil to know when to communicate with the home. Help the parents to respond positively to each success the pupil achieves.
- In case of doubt, or when problems arise, always consult the year head.

For discussion

- Evaluate these guidelines. How helpful do you find them?
- What might you want to add or change if you want to introduce this approach in your own year or house?
- How do you overcome the issue of the demand, in terms of time and commitment, that this approach makes on teachers, who are already pressurized by the system?
- How do you get enough volunteers to make a mentoring scheme viable?

YOUR ROLE IN MONITORING PUPIL PROGRESS AND CO-ORDINATING THE SYSTEM

You receive a great deal of information about the pupils for whom you hold pastoral responsibility. CATs, Yellis and SAT scores are just a part of this information. Each school uses the computer programmes most suited to its needs, or the one which is selected by the local authority for its schools. You may find that the data comes to you in different forms and that you have to spend time making the different programmes compatible. How much technical assistance you get for this varies and this can make your job easy or very difficult indeed. Nevertheless, a major part of your role as the director of the pupil's studies is to be able to interpret the data and use the information it provides about a pupil's potential or progress to support the pupil in his/her studies. The most significant way in which your role as a pastoral manager has developed is that, as the director of the pupil's learning programme, you have to be able to use the information to make projections about what the pupil could achieve. You have to be able to help the student set targets, which will help him/her raise his/her attainment. Ideally your help enables the pupil to exceed those targets. You also have responsibility, either personally or through your use of your tutor team, for monitoring the student's progress towards the targets.

TARGET SETTING

Target setting is one of the current buzz words. If it is to benefit the student and contribute to the raising of achievement, you need to be clear about:

- what target setting means;
- how the targets will be recorded;
- how both the teachers and the students will find the time to do it;
- how progress will be monitored.

Target setting is about defining the logical next step for the student to achieve.

Types of target

1 SMART targets

All targets must be *specific, measurable, achievable, resourced, time-related* (SMART). Simply saying to a pupil *'Try to improve your work'* is not helpful, whereas *'Mary, your target is to finish the next piece of work on time'* or *'Ian, if you label your diagrams, you will get more marks for them. This is something you should remember to do in the next assignment ...'* the target is specific, achievable and time related. It is easy for the teacher to check that the pupil has met the target.

2 Outcome and process targets

Outcome targets: Examples	Process targets: Examples
Raise proportion of students scoring above 85% on NFER reading test to 90%	Implement new more regular assessment and early intervention
Improve attendance rates to a minimum of 94%	Provide daily clerical assistance time for phoning homes of absent students
Raise average grade in science by 0.5 in the next 2 years	Develop more effective teaching strategies in KS4
Raise proportion of boys achieving A/B grades in French at GCSE by 7–10%	Experiment with single-gender teacher at KS4
Raise proportion of students achieving Level 6 or better in the KS3 science test by 10%	Develop and introduce new materials to extend the most able students in science

3   Target zones

Zone	
The historic zone	Continuing as 'We have always done, maintaining the status quo'
The comfort zone	Without much effort we could improve things a bit
The smart/realistic zone	We could make a significant improvement if we changed things
The unlikely/visionary zone	In our wildest dreams, we think our students could achieve this

4   Types of outcome target

Type	
Elite targets	Target a specific group of students (e.g. raising the proportion of students gaining $5 + $ A–C grades at GCSE)
Whole group or average targets	Raising attainment across a cohort (e.g. raising the average points score at GCSE)
Reliability targets	Reducing the number of failing students (e.g. reducing the number of students failing to achieve five A–C grades)

Principles

- Ensure a balance between process targets and outcome targets.
- Do not set too many outcome targets.
- Set targets in the right 'zone'.
- Make sure that the targets are appropriate to your faculty/subject/year group.
- Make sure that target/action/monitoring process and planning is joined up.
- Use a variety of data and be aware of its limitations.
- Set targets with people, not for people.

CASE STUDY 11.10

For reflection

A target-setting initiative at Milestone High School

Target setting (pastoral) – draft plan/discussion document aims:

1. to raise achievement through the active use of target setting;
2. to involve the form tutor in the process;
3. to involve parents in regular review sessions;
4. to motivate the student by providing strategies to meet the targets;
5. to be able to reward those students who achieve targets;
6. to assist the identification of students who are underachieving;
7. to support the academic target setting already established in the school.

Responsibility of:

Heads of year, deputy heads of year, form tutors.
Co-ordinated by: Deputy head (pastoral)

Process

Target-setting days will occur twice within the school year to provide individual interview times. A different day will be used for each year group so that the normal timetable can operate for all other year groups. Some money is available from the raising achievement project (RAP) to buy supply cover, but there is not enough to pay for all the cover needed. Subject teachers freed from lessons or members of the SMT will take classes for the tutors involved in target-setting interviews.

Using the analysis of the first review of aims (RoA):

- follow up procedures in line with current practice;
- form tutors interview students and set three general targets with actions. These targets are recorded on the target sheets;
- parents and teachers are informed of the targets.

Review follows the second RoA of the year:

- review of process – is it working?;
- review of targets and actions;
- renegotiate targets and actions.

Resource implications

Time – some supply cover is paid for via the RAP (see below); if we need more, then we must consider how we can resource it.

Training costs – providing INSET for HoYs and for form tutors. Time for this can be allocated on in-service days. We have to decide whether we have sufficient expertise to do the training in-house or whether we must buy in INSET provision. The cost would be worth it to ensure succeess.

Paper and other materials – trivial.

Associated projects

RAP – raising achievement project – is aimed at years 10 and 11 and is now in its third year in association with our local TEC. The funding has been reduced this year but is available for:

1. target setting – time for HoYs/tutors to support individual students who are under-achieving to set targets, monitor and link with parents;

2. to provide a counsellor on two half-days per week to work with pupils who are under stress, or whose attendance is giving cause for concern.

UA Trust – this is a new project which aims to help underachieving boys. It is a mentoring project, working in partnership with local business and community, and will target particularly those boys at risk of getting into trouble. We hope that, as well as supporting our pupils, this project will help us with strategies for supporting and motivating these pupils.

Timescale for implementation

Spring term:

- INSET for HoY and deputy HoYs;
- presentation of this draft policy to governors for approval.

Summer term:

- INSET for all staff on the designated training day;
- target-setting days included in school calendar for the next academic year.

Autumn term:

- project introduced to parents through an information evening;
- first target-setting day – October 1.

Evaluation:

- analysis of extent to which targets are being met in each year group – are they having the desired effect? (half-yearly HoY);
- feedback from students and parents – after half-year, and at end of first year of the initiative;
- Half-yearly report to governors (pastoral deputy).

Case Study 11.11 illustrates how one school records its targets.

Case Study 11.11

Exemplar of a target sheet

Tracking and target setting

Exemplar of a Y11 tracking record sheet at Southern Cross Technology College

---

Pupil's name   *Form:*

CAT scores: Please tick when you have checked them:

Report grades:

Year 7:

Year 8:

Year-9 progress:

Year-9 report:

Year-9 National Curriculum levels in core subjects

	Teacher assessment	Test result
English		
Mathematics		
Science		

Yellis scores and band checked: please tick when you have checked them:

Report grades:

Year-10 progress:

Year-10 report grades:

Year-11 progress:

Estimated GCSE grades:

	Y10 summer	Y11 progress	After mocks	Y11 progress
No. A*–Cs				
No. A*–Gs				

OTHER RELEVANT INFORMATION

CASE STUDY 11.12

Using the available data to help set appropriate targets

Suppose that one year-11 student's grades for a number of pieces of work during the first term of GCSE. The grades that this student is achieving range between B in the most recent examination, and D. Grade D is the most frequent grade scored.

How should you use a graph or grade plotter to help a student improve his/her performance?

This tracking sheet indicates that this student's target should be to try to improve in the first instance from D to at least C grades. Improving Ds to Cs is an ongoing thrust in schools at the present time. It is not simply a matter of setting a target, however, as without analysis of why the student is performing in this way you may not be able to offer worthwhile guidance. Some pupils struggle with the work because they do not understand the concepts and have not grasped the skills required. Often they do not like to ask basic questions which could make them appear slow or stupid in the eyes of the teacher or their peers. Others spend all their out-of-school time on paid work (e.g. at the local supermarket) and others again are not motivated by the academic programme or by this particular subject. You should work out what the issues are that need to be discussed, but the discussion should be managed by the pupil's tutor or mentor. You do not have the time to handle all the interviews yourself, and it would not be the best use of your time to try to do so. You should only handle the really difficult interviews. This will probably mean that you have to provide training for your tutors or for the team of mentors in how to probe into the factors affecting the pupil's performance, and how to use the information in a way that will make the pupil want to move forward.

The student's tutor or mentor will have to discuss with the student, what the core of the problem is and why s/he is mainly scoring Ds, including a D for course work, when s/he can score a B in the most recent examination. This does looks like a case of the student not working as hard as s/he could, but only talking it through with the student will show you whether it is true. You also need to compare the tracking sheet for this subject with the student's performance in his/her other GCSE subjects. Is s/he scoring mainly Ds in all subjects or just in this one?

CASE STUDY 11.13

Exemplar of a grade plotter

Autumn term

	A*	A	B	C	D	E	F	G	U
Homework Assignment 1					×				
Class Assignment 1				×		×			
Test 1					×				
Coursework 1					×				
Homework Assignment 2					×				
Class Assignment 2						×			
Test 2				×					
Class Assignment 3					×				
Test 3				×					
Coursework 2					×				
Examinations			×						

As a result of his/her session with the pupil, the tutor/mentor can negotiate targets for the next half-term.

For reflection/discussion

- What are the advantages of a grade plotter in helping a student set targets?
- How does this exemplar compare with the practice in your school?

CASE STUDY 11.14

Exemplar

Pupil record sheet

Pupil's name:

Date of interview: Interview no.:

Summary of progress so far (Review of targets):

Overall goal:

Agreed targets for development (maximum of three):

1.

2.

3.

What the pupil will do to make sure that all the targets are met:

Help required from form tutor/mentor:

Signature: Student   Signature: Form tutor/mentor

If you are working to improve student commitment you may want to use a record sheet for this, which is distinct from the target sheet. An example appears below as Case Study 11.15.

CASE STUDY 11.15

Exemplar – for discussion

Student commitment form – years 10 and 11

What do I want to achieve at GCSE?

What do I have to do to achieve my aims?

What are my strengths in achieving this?

What weaknesses will I have to overcome?

What time am I willing to commit to achieving my aim?

What help do I require from my tutor/mentor?

What help do I require from subject teachers? Be specific here (i.e. write about subjects individually).

For discussion

With your tutor team and for them to discuss with the students:

- Does it fulfil its purpose?
- Do they want to modify the sheets (e.g. by adding or changing the questions)?
- How regularly should it be reviewed?
- Should it be signed and by whom?
- Should there be a similar form for the parents?
- How could it be integrated into a weekly planner?
- What procedure should be set up to make contact with the subject teacher/HoD about the answers to the final question?

CASE STUDY 11.16

For action

The tutor brings you this report because he is very concerned. He points out a number of problems. Most of the subject reports now have a clear skills checklist, which both the pupil and teacher tick and which is used as a basis for identifying what the pupil should do to try to improve. This report has no such list and no mention is made in the report of any subject-specific skills. To make matters worse, the tutor feels that not only is the pupil's behaviour unsatisfactory in this subject, but that, even though the pupil promises to try to be more attentive, there is no genuine dialogue here.

This is what the report says:

Half-year RoA

Name: Warren Jones   Form: 9B   Subject: Information technology

Pupil's comments:

I enjoyed working on the assignment. I found out quite a lot about computers - much more than I knew before.

Teacher's comments:

You make very little effort in this lesson. Unfortunately, you disturb the class with your loud and unpleasant behaviour. The result of this is that you have learnt very little in class and that you have held back the standard of the class through your constant interruptions.

Target:

My target is to pay more attention in class. W. B.

For action

- What are the management issues raised in this case study?
- What advice do you give the tutor in handling this situation?
- What part should you play in dealing with it?

CASE STUDY 11.17

For action

You are the head of year 10 and you become aware that Myra Mystry has lost weight this term, and is looking generally anxious. You consult the tutor, but she says that Myra is her usual hardworking self, perhaps a bit quieter than usual, though she is never exuberant. No one, says the tutor, has mentioned any particular problems. It is always difficult to get Myra to confide, so you are not surprised that she has not asked for help. You ask the tutor to put out a 'round robin' to Myra's subject teachers as a check on her progress and to give you a lever into any discussion. The 'round robin' reveals that the teachers are rather concerned about Myra. They cannot fault her effort. Her work is detailed and always beautifully presented. She has been in top sets all the way up the school and identified as a potentially good GCSE candidate. Now, as her GCSE courses get under way, the teachers are beginning to suspect that her results are gained by effort and learning by heart what she has been told in class by the teachers or other pupils. There is no real spark and written assignments lack depth and sometimes indicate a real lack of understanding. If they speak to Myra she insists that she will try harder and do better next time. At first, when you speak to Myra she denies there is a problem, but when you talk about her results in recent tests she becomes very tearful. She is unhappy because she is not succeeding, and because her peers and her teachers can see that she is not doing well. She is terrified of how her parents will react to her report. Myra is the oldest child and the family is very proud of her achievements so far. She does not know what more she can do to improve. She is working until at least midnight every night.

For action

- What are the management issues raised by this case study?
- How do you help Myra to deal with her problem?
- What targets would it be sensible to set for Myra to help her improve?

The subject teachers responded to the 'round robin', but no subject teacher had approached the tutor or you to share his/her concerns about Myra. How can you improve liaison between subject teachers and the pastoral team in order that this kind of information reaches you sooner?

CASE STUDY 11.18

For action

Liam is very articulate. He can be difficult to handle in class because he enjoys putting the other point of view and taking on the teachers, but, reluctantly, they concede that his arguments are always logical and can be good. He is much less keen to put his thoughts on paper and avoids homework whenever possible. For sometime his intelligence was underestimated. Indeed, during years 7 and 8 he was given special-needs support, which you now suspect that he didn't really need. He did well in the SATs at the end of Key Stage 3, and has the potential to be a strong GCSE candidate if he were sufficiently motivated.

For action

You are the head of year 10.
- What are the issues raised in this case study?
- What do you do to prevent Liam from becoming a disaffected troublemaker and to help him achieve his potential?

BIBLIOGRAPHY AND FURTHER READING

George, D. (1997) Haringay Education Department.
Powell, R. (1997) *Raising Achievement*, Stafford: Robert Powell Publications.
Terrel, I., Rowe, S. and Terrell, K. (1997) *Raising Achievement at GCSE, A Practical Guide for Subject Departments*, Lancaster: Framework Press.

Index